First in my Family

How Parents Can Support College Achievement

Elizabeth Dayton

Charles Dayton

Foothill Associates
Nevada City, CA 95959
ISBN 0997946709
ISBN-13 978-0997946703

To my parents

For providing the very first data to motivate this book:
You've offered indisputable evidence that strong family relationships can support children in achieving their dreams;
here's looking at three decades and counting.

-E.H.D.

Contents

Page

List of Figures vii
Prologue 1
Chapter 1: What Is This Book About? 3
Chapter 2: Is College Worth It? 13
Chapter 3: Who Goes To College? 33
Chapter 4: Social Capital—The Lynchpin 47
Chapter 5: Parenting Styles 57
Chapter 6: Family Relationships Matter 79
Chapter 7: Falling Short of College 95
Chapter 8: Conclusions and Implications 107
References 129
Appendix 143
Acknowledgements 157
About the Authors 159

Figures

Page

Figure 1: Educational attainment in America 34
Figure 2: Educational attainment among kids whose parents achieved less than high school, high school, some college, and bachelors educations...................36
Figure 3: Educational attainment among quartiles of family income...37
Figure 4: Gender of students who reach no college, some college, and four-year college................................38
Figure 5: Race/ethnicity of students who reach no college, some college, and four-year college........................39
Figure 6: Percent of students with above-average family incomes who follow each intergenerational educational path...41
Figure 7: Percent of female and male students who follow each intergenerational educational path..................42
Figure 8: Race/ethnicity of students who follow each intergenerational educational path........................43
Figure 9: Educational attainment disaggregated by family relationships...80
Figure 10: The odds of being a first-generation some-college student with each family relationship...............86
Figure 11: The odds of being a first-generation bachelor with each family relationship..................................87
Figure 12: The odds of being a some-college legacy with each family relationship..................................92
Figure 13: The odds of being a bachelor's legacy with each family relationship..92
Figure 14: Family relationships for youth who follow each intergenerational educational path........................97
Figure 15: Reduced odds of falling short of some-college..........98
Figure 16: Reduced odds of falling short of four-year college.....98

Prologue

About one in three young people in the United States completes a bachelor's degree, and a similar proportion earns a college education shy of a bachelor's degree, such as an associate's degree, certification, or simply completion of some postsecondary courses. While this number has edged up a bit in recent years, the vast majority of American youth desire to attend college, and their parents wish the same for them. Millions fall short of their goal.

To shed light on how families can support children's college attainment, I analyzed a large national dataset and discovered that across the board, supportive family relationships had a striking statistical effect on young people going to college—in families with heaps of education or very little, for daughters and for sons, regardless of aptitude, immigrant status, or family income.

These findings spoke to ways that parents might encourage their children's educations simply by spending time with them and supporting their interests, which doesn't require first-hand understanding of college or mountains of money. Indeed, supportive family relationships are largely free, and are available at least in principle to virtually every family.

Over the course of conducting this research I also talked with hundreds of people about the role their family played in supporting their educational achievements (or not—this isn't *everyone's* story). Statistics are invaluable but they can also be dry; as human beings we like stories. So I sought out first-generation college students to exemplify what I had found in my statistical analyses, to include their stories alongside the nationally representative statistics.

This book is, essentially, a recasting of my research as a doctoral student at Johns Hopkins University and a postdoctoral fellow at Stanford University. However, I have not written this book alone. A few years ago I shared my research on how parenting supports college achievement with my Dad, Charlie, and he encouraged me to translate it into a book. While it was full of information we both thought would be valuable to families across the country, it was written in an academic style, with technical terminology and countless footnotes. I loved the idea, but between my postdoctoral work and the arrival of my first child the book project kept getting pushed aside. Given Charlie's decades of experience in educational research and love of writing (see "About the Authors"), we arrived at the idea to form a new partnership to make this book happen, with Charlie "translating" my academic research into more conversational language. Given the research subject, the father-daughter collaboration seemed particularly apt.

For the sake of simplicity, and because the book is based on my original research, I serve as the narrative voice. Charlie's contributions were Chapter 2, which presents a discussion of the headline issues in college-going today such as the rising cost of college, student debt, and how the value of a college education has changed over time; Chapter 8's concluding discussion of how schools and communities can use this book to better support students to achieve a college education; and simplifying my academic writing into something hopefully a little more fun for a general audience to read.

Chapter 1

What Is This Book About?

Most young people in America want to go to college. It's a core element of the American Dream. Ask any parent and they'll almost surely say, "Yes, of course I want my child to go to college." For some, this is accompanied by a secure nod: "And you can be sure it's going to happen." For others, it's more likely to be a sad shrug: "Sure, it would be nice, but let's be realistic, we probably can't make it happen."

There's a good reason a college education is part of the American Dream. College opens many opportunities, including greater earning potential and access to more advanced careers. There is also real value to the learning that goes on there, and notable prestige to being able to say you have a college degree.

In the last few years increasingly frequent articles in the popular press and TV have challenged the value of college given rising costs, growing debt, and the changing economy. I'll examine each of these issues in the next chapter, "Is College Worth It?" Spoiler alert: the answer is a resounding "Yes." By *many* meaningful measures college is more valuable today than ever before. Yet only about one-third of today's students achieve the dream of earning a bachelor's degree, and only another third or so earns an associate's degree, postsecondary certificate, or attends some college shy of a degree.

Some of the reasons for this gap between the dreams young people and their families have and the realities they face seem obvious. College can be hard to get into; students need good grades and test scores. They need to be able to pay for it, and the trends of the last couple of decades show that college costs have risen substantially.

Another factor is family history. If a young person's parents didn't go to college—if there is no family history of college going—there is likely to be less focus on this goal, and less understanding of how to achieve it. This has been illustrated in work such as Annette Lareau's groundbreaking book *Unequal Childhoods: Class, Race, and Family Life* (2011); a report from the Higher Education Research Institute titled *First in my family: A profile of first-generation college students at four-year institutions since 1971* (Saenz et al 2007); and research out of the National Center for Education Statistics titled *Students whose parents did not go to college: Postsecondary access, persistence, and attainment* (Choy 2001). For young people from families without a history of attending college, a college degree can seem more like a hazy mirage on some distant horizon than a destination at the end of a clearly-defined path with well-marked signposts. This too is often a barrier.

So maybe it comes down to what pretty much every other social outcome seems to be linked to, *socioeconomic status*. In brief, *SES*. Most sociologists and educators who study the statistics will tell you that educational outcomes have a lot to do with SES. How is SES defined? Generally by family income and level of education. If the parents completed college and make good money, they're high SES. If they neither went to college nor have high incomes, they're low SES. Of course there are lots of gradations of both of these factors—income and education exist along a spectrum—but the essential index includes these two factors.

So there you have it. College is hard to get into, costs a lot, and isn't likely to happen unless the parents went. Following that logic, young people's futures are pretty much determined by the time they are born, by their family's SES and factors beyond their control.

But do *any* young people make it past these daunting barriers? Maybe a few? There are always a few exceptions to rules. But how many? Maybe ten percent of kids become the first in their family to attend college? Five? Less?

Surprisingly, the answer is...*twenty-six percent!* Yes, one out of every four young people becomes the first in their family to attend either any college or a four-year college. What explains this degree of upward mobility? That's the very question that led to this book: What is going on for the twenty-six percent of young people who become the first generation in their family to attend college? Can we learn anything by studying how they were different?

There's another half to this question: If twenty-six percent of young people overcome some really big barriers, what about those who don't have those barriers, the young people with parents who *have* college degrees. Of course we assume they all *go* to college, right? Well, again, except for maybe a few. But how many don't attend college?

That number is...*twenty-four percent!* Nearly the same number of young people that surpass their parents' education to become the first generation to attend college *fail* to attend college in spite of their parents' higher education. Their parents went to college, and presumably wanted them to also, but they didn't.

If we put these two numbers together, we see that fully one-half of young people follow a different educational trajectory than their parents: a quarter become the first generation in their family to attend college, while another quarter fail to replicate their parents' college attainment. This is a striking amount of educational mobility, and it belies the stereotype that "It all comes down to SES."

How are we to understand all this educational mobility? Since this book is based on sociological research, it rests on terminology used in sociology. In this parlance, it is valuable to define a few key phrases: "human capital," "financial capital," and "social capital." A college education can be thought of as creating "human capital," which includes the benefits of getting a college education, and an understanding of how higher education works. Human capital is basically captured by level of education. Parents with college degrees, or at least some college experience, can share this human capital with their children.

Next comes "financial capital," which is essentially level of income. Given the relationship between education and career opportunities, it's not surprising that a family's human and financial capital are highly correlated. That is, a young person who comes from a family with college-educated parents probably also comes from one with a solid income. Contrastingly, someone who grows up in a family without any college in its history probably also faces some financial challenges.

What about "social capital?" Social capital refers to the value of human interactions, or in this context, supportive family relationships. This, too, tends to correlate with the other forms of capital. Young people with more-educated, higher-income parents are more likely to share the kinds of family relationships that promote education. Contrastingly, children with less-educated, lower-income parents are less likely to do so. Again, Lareau (2002), Choy (2001), and Saenz's (2007), as well as Melvin Kohn (1966), have done interesting work that speaks to this finding. But if all of these forms of capital tend to come as a bundle, then why are a quarter of young people upwardly mobile, and another quarter downwardly mobile?

Let me introduce James Coleman (1926-1995), whose work shaped educational theory and policy across the second half of the twentieth century. He theorized that supportive family relationships (i.e., social capital) are important for children's educational attainment. In fact, he argued that human capital (parent education) must be accompanied by social capital (supportive family relationships) in order to influence children's attainment. Without strong relationships, there is no mechanism through which to transmit the benefits of human capital from one generation to the next. That is, unless parents share their understanding of higher education their advantage will not be passed down.

In Coleman's view, social capital is the lynchpin. Without it, those other advantages don't much matter. But this was just a theory. Without hard statistical evidence, it's difficult to know why fifty percent of young people diverge from their parents' educational path. Which brings me to the research that underlies this book. How might these theories be tested? How are you going to gather enough information from enough families over a long enough period of time to really look at whether family relationships are related to all this educational mobility?

It turns out there is a database called the National Longitudinal Survey of Youth 1997 (hereafter referred to as NLSY97), which provides a picture of American youth's attitudes, experiences, characteristics, and outcomes over a long period of time. Sponsored by the U.S. Bureau of Labor Statistics, the NLSY97 is a representative survey of young people across the United States who were ages 12 to 16 on December 31, 1996. These same youth have been surveyed again every year since. In research parlance, it's a "nationally representative" and "longitudinal" survey.

By design, 13 and 14 year-olds were asked questions that best tap into family relationships, such as how supportive, responsive, and directive their parents are; whether their parents know their friends, friends' parents, teachers, whereabouts, and school activities; and whether there are frequent family conversations about education and goals. This book follows these 13 and 14 year-olds through ages 23-24 (from 1997 through 2007), when I examined their college attainment. This is a meaningful span of years, since according to the National Center for Education Statistics (2008) bachelor's degrees are typically earned by ages 22-24 in the United States. However, the book examines both bachelor's degrees *and* other college experiences (e.g., two-year college and discontinued college attendance shy of a degree) to allow for an understanding of the role of family relationships in various postsecondary paths.

A full description of the statistical methodology used to analyze the NLSY97 is presented in the Appendix. This includes a listing of the dependent and independent variables, the forms of statistical analyses performed (primarily multinomial logistic regression), and other important statistical considerations. Suffice it to say here that this was sophisticated, and advised by leaders in the field.

It is important to understand, however, that this research is what statisticians call "observational," which means that it does not warrant "causal inference." That is, while the findings presented in the following pages apply to youth from all levels of family income and academic aptitude, for girls and boys, those with ancestors on the Mayflower and new immigrants, and for *everyone,* statistically it is still not certain that supportive family relationships are the driving force behind the findings. The reason for this is that causal inference requires a research design unavailable here: random assignment. No one can randomly assign youth to one family or another. Given this, I analyzed the data every way I could imagine to make sure the statistical relationships between family interactions and youths' achievements were strong. I "controlled" for every factor that seemed like it might affect this, including:

- Family income
- Parent educational level
- Student aptitude
- Immigrant status
- Race/ethnicity
- Gender

This means that every time I cite a statistical difference, it can't be explained by any of these factors. Across family incomes, parent educational levels, student aptitudes, immigrant statuses, races/ethnicities, and genders, the findings presented in this book hold.

Nevertheless, it is possible that other factors remain that I wasn't able to analyze and that are associated with both family relationships and educational success. In my academic writing, I am careful to avoid causal language (e.g., I will say that supportive family relationships "predict" children's educational success rather than "cause" it). In this book, aimed at a more general audience, I have opted for less technical language: I have written that "supportive family relationships *matter* for children's educational success," and I'm going to rely on you to remember that while my statistical findings are strong, they are based on observational data and therefore are not necessarily causal.

That said, this book is founded on solid statistics. That is one of the primary reasons I felt compelled to make it available to a broader audience. This research presents an abundance of data and statistically significant findings that bear on the kinds of ideas that James Coleman speculated about. The purpose of writing the book was to translate the findings into clear enough terms that a wide audience could understand them and benefit from them.

Throughout the book I illustrate what I found with personal stories gathered from interviews with first-generation college students. These excerpts come word-for-word from conversations with fourteen first-generation college students.

I met these students through personal networks and an organization designed to support first-generation students. We talked on campus, in cafes, and by phone for forty-five minutes to two hours during 2014-2015. Interviewees were diverse: they were female and male; White, Black, Hispanic, Asian, and American Indian; and from every major region of the United States. Most attended an elite university, though they included students from state colleges, state universities, and less competitive private colleges. Alongside quotes I've indicated students' gender, race/ethnicity, and where they were from to give you some sense for who they are. However, I've omitted other characteristics to protect students' anonymity, especially given the relatively small sample. I have also omitted or subtly changed potentially identifying characteristics within quotes (again to protect anonymity), yet taking care not to change the meaning of students' stories.

The interviews themselves were conversations, casual and intimate. To begin an interview, I described my statistical findings, then asked how their experiences aligned with what I was seeing in the data: What kinds of opportunities for family interaction did they have? What was the tone of interactions? The substance? Questions came up in a different order depending on the flow of conversation, but what I sought were specific stories illustrating how these first-generation students' families worked: how families interacted, what their relationships were like, and whether they reflected what I was seeing in my analyses.

These interviews were conducted precisely to illustrate my broad national statistical findings. They were conducted to make the book more readable, to render it more accessible, to bring the statistical findings to life. A single student's statement is present in each highlighted box. To begin with one student's words…

In their own words:
How I became a first-generation college student
from a Hispanic female from the South

Thinking about my high school graduation…I get chills just thinking about it. It was one of the most rewarding experiences I've had, just seeing my parents' faces in the stadium. I was in the front row so I could see them well. And they were just staring at me the whole time, just glossy-eyed staring at me. I had never felt anything like that. I mean, I knew my parents were proud, but after that day it kind of solidified.

I did a lot of introspection throughout high school, realizing how many sacrifices my parents were making for me, and seeing their willingness to do whatever they could for me to get what I needed to have. I was never spoiled in the usual sense, but I was extremely spoiled in the sense that my parents had such determination to get me through high school. Not a lot of my friends had support from their parents like that.

It would be easy to say that my parents didn't support me academically because they hadn't learned what I was studying in school. But the emotional support was very significant. I remember the late nights. Sometimes my Mom would come and just sit with me at two in the morning as I was reading. She would even come and just sleep on the bed to keep me company. And just having her there was incredible.

I feel so lucky, but it's also really hard to hear from my college classmates about all their other resources, their private high schools and tutors, and their parents doing everything for them. But I guess what I have instead is the pride that I managed to do this quote-unquote "on my own," just because I didn't have the same kind of help.

Though my pride is also a pride for my parents, it's actually not just my own. I really see my achievement as theirs, too. I've said it before: when I graduated high school my Dad felt as though he graduated with me, and so did my Mom. I remember my Dad immediately after graduation when we went home wanted to wear my cap and hold my diploma and take a picture. And I see that picture and it fills my heart with so much joy to know that I did this for him.

Now that I'm at college, what powers me through is to remember my Dad's face at my high school graduation. Now I want to see my Dad's face at my college graduation. It's definitely something that pushes me forward.

It gets hard and it gets intimidating being at college with kids who had so much more, but I'm so proud of what my family went through to get me here. And when I'm biking around campus, when for a second I take my mind off the place I need to be and what I need to do and just look around, I still just think: "Wow, I'm at college!" I'm excited when I see my college logo on a trashcan! It's crazy! It's real!

The outline of the book

Chapter 2 addresses the public debate raging around the value of a college education with a close, hard look at the question of whether and to what degree college is worth it today. Among the topics covered are increasing costs and levels of student debt, trends over time, how important choosing a major is, and both the financial and nonfinancial benefits of a college degree.

Chapter 3 presents nationally representative data detailing who goes to college, looking at how many young people make it to what level, from less than high school completion to a graduate or professional degree. Then it shows how these outcomes relate to family education and income levels, as well as gender and race/ethnicity.

Chapter 4 offers an overview of previous research findings about the influence of family resources on educational outcomes, looking at the three dimensions of family resources that James Coleman defined: human, financial, and social capital. The first two of these usually defines socioeconomic status: parent education and family income. But it's the third, social capital, and specifically the influence of family relationships, that is of particular interest here. This chapter explores various aspects of social capital, providing examples of how it functions, and offering many insights into how almost any family can support children's achievements.

Chapter 5 looks at different parenting styles. I've broken these into three dimensions: opportunities for family interaction, the tone of interactions, and the substance of interactions. These are operationally defined, as a lead-in to the book's central original findings, which are presented in Chapters 6 and 7.

Chapter 6 shows what I have discovered about the importance of family relationships for youth's educational achievements, including the effects of each of the three aspects of family relationships discussed in Chapter 5: opportunities for interactions, their tone, and the degree of substance they have. These findings are the heart of this book—they are the original discoveries that can empower parents to support children's educations even without the benefit of having a college education or high income themselves.

Chapter 7 looks at *downward* mobility: the quarter of young people who fail to replicate their parent's college achievements, and what family relationships have to do with children's downward mobility. Here too parents may be empowered to protect their children's achievements by sharing strong relationships.

Finally, Chapter 8 provides a recap of findings presented throughout the book, and offers a discussion of their implications for public policy and future research.

Chapter 2

Is College Worth It?

In recent years many people have questioned the value of a college education. This is especially true of the traditional four-year degree. Critics generally agree that *some* education beyond high school is useful; they just question whether the quickly spiraling costs of four-year degree programs justify their expense in terms of future earnings. Such critics note that two-year degrees, or often just some coursework that provides skills needed in a particular industry or career, are considerably cheaper and often as useful.

The question has become: Are bachelor's degrees a relic of the past? Many factors bear on this question. For example:

- A lot of statistics get thrown around in this discussion. Which ones are reliable?

- In examining the question of whether college is beneficial, have things changed from the past? Is a four-year college degree an anachronism? Is a two-year degree, or even a briefer certification, as good as a bachelor's degree when it comes to employment and earnings?

- Rising student debt is an important part of this discussion. How big a problem is it?

- Going to college is one thing, but choosing a major *in* college is something else. How important is the choice of major?

- There are a lot of colleges out there, some with much bigger reputations than others. Is getting into a competitive college what's really important?

- Will a college education truly level the playing field for first-generation students, or is this just an illusion? What happens after college for such students?

- Are there non-financial outcomes that matter, and reasons to attend college from other standpoints, or is it all just about future earnings?

Postsecondary education of most kinds brings measurable advantages. The original research presented in this book looks at *both* four-year college and some-college paths. This chapter will not advocate that a four-year degree is the only or even the best option for everyone; huge benefits can be gained from all kinds of postsecondary education. According to statistics from the National Center for Education Statistics from 2014, community colleges now enroll about 40% of postsecondary students and offer an immense range of courses and opportunities. Not only do they provide concrete employment-related training useful for entering or bettering careers in any number of fields, they also offer a less expensive way to obtain the first two years of academic courses for those wanting a four-year degree. Similar things can be said of many trade schools. While there are cautions to be aware of regarding for-profit institutions, like learning about placement rates and earnings of graduates and debt levels students typically take on, many are beneficial. However, the discussion in this chapter focuses on four-year programs, partly because that is where the largest proportion of students attend college, and partly because that is where the front-page discussion has centered.

Whose Statistics Should You Believe?

Let's take the questions in the order presented above, beginning with which statistics are reliable. The old saying that "Statistics don't lie, but liars use statistics" is pretty much on the money. It's possible to argue almost any viewpoint with what seem like persuasive numbers.

A host of articles in recent years has addressed the growing costs of four-year colleges, and national newspapers seem to include this topic almost weekly. Let's begin by taking a look at the kinds of statistics that bear on the discussion of college costs. One important concept to understand here is inflation, which is the amount *all* costs increase over time. We all remember our parents or grandparents complaining about how much prices have gone up. "I used to be able to buy a hamburger for fifty cents" or "My grandfather talked about buying a new car for three thousand dollars." While these statements are true, what they ignore is the average incomes in those times. A three thousand dollar car sounds cheap today, but if average incomes were only a tenth as much back then, the cost of cars isn't all that different today. What about college costs?

No one can contend that costs haven't been rising, and faster than inflation, as measured by the typical comparison figures such as the "Cost-of-Living Index" or "Consumer Price Index," two measures that reflect the effects of inflation. While the statistical data that go into such calculations are complex, they show that inflation has increased the cost of most things by a substantial amount over the past twenty years. To use one relatively simple measure, let's consider the figure the United States government uses to calculate an annual cost-of-living adjustment (COLA) for Social Security benefits. From 1992-2012 this increased an average of about 2.6% per year, or a total of ~52% over those 20 years. This means that something that cost $100 in 1992 would have cost $152 in 2012, simply from the effects of inflation, the reduced value of the dollar.

How have college costs changed during this period? Inflation-adjusted data from the College Board, spanning 1993-94 through 2013-14, reveal a mixed picture:

- Two-year college costs have increased an average of about 2.5 percent per year, or 50 percent across these two decades
- Public four-year costs have increased about 4 percent per year, for a total of 80 percent
- Private four-year costs, while substantially higher than two-year or public four-year costs, have increased by about 2.7 percent per year, for a total of

a 54 percent increase

If we were to ignore inflation across these twenty years, these cost increases would all appear to be about 50% higher. When newspapers report that college costs have more than doubled recently, that's in inflated dollars. Much of that seemingly huge jump is from inflation.

Still drawing on data from the College Board, 2013-14 average costs for tuition and fees across four years at public colleges averaged about $35,000, and at private colleges (the most expensive category) about $120,000. Two-year public colleges were much less expensive, averaging about $6,500. And room and board must be added to these figures for most four-year colleges. But while this certainly doesn't make college inexpensive, college costs are often presented as much higher, based on what elite schools charge, such as the Ivy League colleges. Those numbers do not represent averages. Sure, you can pay $100,000 for a high-end car also, even though the average cost is more like $30,000. Just don't be misled about the difference between averages and exceptions. Whether that really expensive school is worth the cost is a topic we'll get to a few pages along.

Another factor is that such comparisons often present just the tuition numbers published in college catalogs and brochures, as opposed to the actual costs to the typical student once financial aid is figured in. The published numbers *will* apply to students from well-off families who don't qualify for assistance, but they are often substantial exaggerations for the rest. Most students benefit from some form of aid, such as scholarships, fellowships, work-study programs and the like. And most colleges offer tuition breaks for families with lower incomes, which are often defined broadly enough to include most middle class families. This is why we have to fill out that government FASFA form when we're figuring out how much a college is actually going to charge us: family income influences how much college actually costs.

An article in the *New York Times* by David Leonhardt entitled "How the Government Exaggerates the Cost of College" (July 29, 2014) captures this point. It discusses the differences between government statistics, which reflect tuition and associated rates published by colleges, and those of the College Board, which factor in student aid. With the latter included, actual increases in annual college costs are roughly halved. Of course this does mean students often have to fulfill certain obligations, such as maintaining a given grade point average to keep an academic scholarship or working a certain amount in a work-study position.

The article also points out that while expenses in other arenas, such as automobiles or high-tech equipment, are subject to foreign competition, which has brought down costs over time, college expenses are almost purely domestic and thus not subject to such competition. This makes comparing the relative increase in college costs with products in other fields somewhat unfair.

Are Bachelor's Degrees Still Worth It?

Let's move on to our second question: Is a four-year college degree an anachronism? Is a two-year degree, or even a briefer certification, as good as a bachelor's degree when it comes to employment and earnings?

Data from the Bureau of Labor Statistics' Current Population Survey (2014) illustrate the impact education has on income. They compare average earnings for full-time wage and salary workers aged 25 and over who have achieved a wide range of educations:

- Less than a high school diploma: $472/week
- High school diploma: $651/week
- Some college, no degree: $727/week
- Associate's degree: $777/week
- Bachelor's degree: $1,108/week
- Master's degree: $1,329/week
- Professional degree: $1,714/week
- Doctoral degree: $1,623/week

The simplest observation here is that as education rises, so do earnings, and by a lot. The $1,108 average weekly earnings for someone with a bachelor's degree is 70% higher than that for someone with only a high school diploma ($651), and 51% higher than for someone with an associate's degree ($777). More advanced degrees extend this advantage further. There is a very clear correlation between higher education and increased salaries. These are of course averages; some such differences will be smaller, and some will be larger.

The same figure also sheds light on education's impact on unemployment for full-time wage and salary workers aged 25 and over:

- Less than a high school diploma: 11% unemployment rate
- High school diploma: 7.5% unemployment rate
- Some college, no degree: 7% unemployment rate
- Associate's degree: 5.4% unemployment rate
- Bachelor's degree: 4% unemployment rate
- Master's degree: 3.4% unemployment rate
- Professional degree: 2.3% unemployment rate
- Doctoral degree: 2.2% unemployment rate

The effect of education on unemployment is also quite clear: across the board, more education is associated with a lower unemployment rate. A bachelor's degree cuts the chances of unemployment roughly in half compared to someone with just a high school diploma. When you add these two factors together—substantially increased incomes and substantially reduced chances of unemployment—the value of education beyond high school, especially at the bachelor's degree level and higher, appears dramatic.

A book entitled "The College Payoff" by Anthony Carnevale, Stephen Rose, and Ban Cheah (2009) at the Georgetown University Center on Education and the Workforce compares average salaries for adults with various levels of education. It reports that the gap between those with a bachelor's degree and just a high school diploma is actually growing. To quote:

> According to the study, individuals with a bachelor's degree now make 84 percent more over a lifetime than those with only a high school diploma, up from 75 percent in 1999. Today, bachelor's degree holders can expect median lifetime earnings approaching $2.3 million. By comparison, workers with just a high school diploma average roughly $1.3 million…

The simple math here is that a college degree results in about a $1 million difference over the average person's lifetime earnings. The authors also point out that such a degree is the gateway to graduate education, which increases the difference further. For example, a master's degree raises the 84% difference to slightly more than double, a doctoral degree makes it two and a half times as much, and a professional degree raises it to 2.8 times as much.

These are pretty clear arguments for more education, and the more the better. A report from the Pew Research Center (2014) also speaks to how the benefits of college today compare to past generations. Written by Paul Taylor, Rick Fry and Russ Oates and entitled "The Rising Cost of Not Going to College," the report bases its analysis on a recent nationally representative survey of 2,002 individuals, supplemented by data from the U.S. Census Bureau. Based on 2013 data, it compares individuals aged 25 to 32 that year (what are often referred to as "Millennials", usually defined as those born after the early 1980s who reached adulthood by 2000) with those from earlier generations.

The report, like the previous one, illustrates not that four-year degrees are becoming *less* valuable, but *more* valuable. That is, the gap in earnings between those with bachelor's degrees and high school degrees is widening. Adjusted for inflation, here are average annual earnings over time:

- In 1965—
    - High school graduates earned $31,384
    - Those with some college earned $33,655
    - Those with a bachelor's degree earned $38,833
- By 1986—
    - High school graduates earned $30,525
    - Those with some college earned $34,595
    - Those with a bachelor's degree earned $44,770
- In 2013—
    - High school graduates earned $28,000
    - Those with some college earned $30,000
    - Those with a bachelor's degree earned $45,500

To sum this up: Across the forty-eight years from 1965 to 2013, young adults with bachelor's degrees came to earn 17% *more*, with (inflation-adjusted) earnings rising from $38,833 to $45,500/year.

By comparison, those with just a high school diploma came to earn 11% *less,* with (inflation-adjusted) earnings actually *falling* from $31,384 to $28,000/year. This means that while in 1965 high school graduates earned 81% of what college graduates earned, a difference of about $7500/year, by 2013, high school graduates earned just 62% of the average bachelor's graduates' earnings, a difference of fully $17,500/year.

The report acknowledges that the so-called "Great Recession" of 2008 hit the Millennial generation particularly hard. In fact, 22% of Millennials with only a high school diploma were living in poverty in 2013, compared to 15% of similarly situated individuals from the previous generation ("Generation X") in 1995, and only 7% of "Baby Boomers" in 1979, when those individuals were in their late twenties and early thirties.

The news was not all bad for Millennials, however. According to the report, Millennials are the best-educated generation in history, as more than one-third (34%) have at least a bachelor's degree, compared to 24% of similarly situated Baby Boomers in the late 1970s and 1980s. As we just saw, those degrees are becoming more valuable because they predict enhanced earnings over a lifetime.

Another factor in calculating the worth of college relates to the changing job market. Compared with the past, today there are relatively few well-paying and rewarding occupations for those with only a high school diploma. While a high school diploma once represented a significant achievement (one hundred years ago only about 15% of any given cohort reached this level), this has faded fast as an adequate benchmark of educational achievement, at least as an entry point for most careers. *Most* occupations now require *some* education beyond high school.

One can get a sense for these changes by looking at what the entry-level options were a couple of generations ago, say in the 1950s-60s. There were lots of jobs then in such fields as farming, construction, and manufacturing that required little more than a strong back and good work ethic. Those are pretty much gone from the American economy. Auto mechanics today, for example, better know something about computers if they want to work on a car manufactured in the last two decades. Farmers better know something about fertilizers, irrigation, complex machinery, and projected crop futures. And building contractors better know a lot more than how to pound a nail or saw a board if they want to understand current building codes and pass today's licensing exams.

While the number of jobs requiring *some* education beyond high school has grown substantially, the number requiring a four-year degree has also grown, and continues to do so. The U.S. Bureau of Labor Statistics projects that from 2012 through 2022 (the most recent numbers available), 19 of the 30 occupations projected to grow fastest typically require some form of postsecondary education for entry. Furthermore, occupations typically requiring postsecondary education for entry generally had higher median wages ($57,770) in 2012 and are projected to grow faster (14.0%) between 2012 and 2022 than occupations that typically require a high school diploma or less ($27,670 and 9.1%).

How Big a Problem Is Student Debt?

Student debt is large and growing. While credit card and car loan debt have been falling in recent years, student loan debt has been rising. This parallels what I've already discussed about college costs: even adjusted for inflation, four-year college costs have risen about 50% over the past two decades. Student debt has followed this trend, and even exceeded it. Just how serious is this? Is it time to declare that college is just too expensive for all but the wealthy, regardless of its benefits? Is it time to steer young people away from pricey four-year bachelor's degree programs and into two-year colleges or technical schools?

First, let's take a closer look at the numbers. Examining data from the U.S. Department of Education's National Postsecondary Student Aid Study, conducted every four years, we see in the most recently available data that in 2012, 71% of all students graduating from four-year colleges had student loan debt. That represents 1.3 million students graduating with debt, up from 1.1 million in 2008 and 0.9 million in 2004. Looking at this student debt by type of college:

- 66% of graduates from public colleges had student loans, averaging $25,550, up from

$20,450 in 2008.
- 75% of graduates from private nonprofit colleges had student loans, averaging $32,300, up from $28,200 in 2008.
- 88% of graduates from for-profit colleges had student loans, averaging $39,950, up from $31,800 in 2008.

This is a lot for many young people to face as they emerge from college, especially if they're having trouble finding a job.

Illustrating the real stress loans can cause, in a *New York Times* piece entitled "Degrees of Debt" (May 12, 2012), Andrew Martin and Andrew Lehren cite the example of a young woman graduating with $120,000 in student loan debt, who is working two jobs and about to move back in with her parents. Both she and her mother, who cosigned the loans, are terrified at the prospect of having to pay back this much money. The authors note that "With more than $1 trillion in student loans outstanding in this country, crippling debt is no longer confined to dropouts from for-profit colleges or graduate students who owe on many years of education, some of the overextended debtors in years past."

It is a problem. Students need to approach borrowing cautiously. As anyone who has had debts to pay off knows all too well, it's easier to borrow money than it is to pay it back. But having said that, note the difference between the example used in this *New York Times* piece and the averages just presented. Getting seriously overextended isn't a wise move; there are real dangers there. But that figure of $120,000 was about four times the national average.

Let's look at this another way. People take out loans for a reason, and one of the best reasons is that they offer an investment that hopefully will more than pay for itself over time. Is there any evidence this is still the case for college degrees? The sentence following the one quoted above from that *New York Times* piece reads: "As prices soar, a college degree statistically remains a good lifetime investment," a statement which seems to contradict the tone of the article.

Does a college degree remain a good lifetime investment? Researchers at the Hamilton Project, launched in 2006 as an economic policy initiative at the Brookings Institution, have looked at this question. In a piece by Adam Looney and Michael Greenstone entitled "Regardless of the Cost, College Still Matters" (2012), they examine that statistical claim.

> The Hamilton Project estimated that investing in a four-year degree yields a return of above 15 percent. While this is down slightly from almost 18 percent in the late '90s, attending college remains one of the best ways one can invest her money. The return to college is more than double the average return over the last 60 years experienced in the stock market (6.8 percent), and more than five times the return to investments in corporate bonds (2.9 percent), gold (2.3 percent), long-term government bonds (2.2 percent), or housing (0.4 percent). ...the claim that college is no longer a sound investment is not rooted in fact. The rate of return has remained relatively constant over the last three decades. If attending college was a good idea in the '80s, it's still a good idea today.

So, where are we? We agree that getting $120,000 in debt is questionable, unless it's to prepare for a very high paying, secure occupation. You should also take a close look at for-profit colleges if you're considering one, to learn just what their placement rates and loan default rates are; that's where the worst of the student debt problem lies, and where students most often (proportionally) get into serious debt trouble.

But let's do the math. If the average debt of graduating college seniors today is approximately $35,000, and the average difference in a young person's (aged 25 to 32) salary between someone with just a high school diploma and someone with a bachelor's degree is about $17,500 (recalling the data from Taylor, Fry and Oates, above), how long is it going to take to gain back the value hoped for from that loan? Two years. And what happens after that, for the next 40 or so years of the average worker's career? An extra $17,500 of income annually. Of course, most students pay off loans in smaller installments over longer periods of time. And those who begin working right out of high school do have a four-year head start on their earnings. But even with these considerations, it doesn't take long for the average bachelor's degree to pay off. To the tune, on average, of about $1 million over a person's lifetime. That's roughly a ten-to-one payoff on the average cost of even a private four-year college degree.

Do Majors Matter?

All these statistics suggest the growing value of postsecondary education and the correlation of education and income all the way up the educational ladder. But we haven't considered yet the focus of that education. Does the major one chooses make a difference? Do those who major in archeology or art generally enjoy similar earnings and stability as those who major in, say, civil engineering or pre-med? Do creative writing or dance majors do as well as, say, software engineering majors? In short, what's the relationship between what you study in college and how well you do as a result?

A 2014 piece in *Higher Ed* by Ben Casselman delves into this question. Entitled "The Economic Guide to Picking a College Major" (September 12, 2014), this analysis provides a table with 173 majors broken down by income. That's a little more than I will cover here, but let's look at some of the key points.

Casselman comes up with a figure of $36,000 as the median annual starting wage of college graduates in 2014. At one end of the spectrum is petroleum engineering, with a median annual starting wage of $110,000 (an outlier, due to the then boom in oil drilling; the second occupation on the list was nearly 50% lower). At the other end is library science, at $22,000. While warning that engineering isn't a guarantee of a high-paying job, given the boom or bust history of many jobs in the category, his analysis gives a powerful nod to this field, where "A remarkable 17 of the 20 highest-paying majors for young graduates fall under… 'engineering.' Even the lowest-paying engineering majors still pay a median wage of $40,000."

Casselman also underscores that while STEM (science, technology, engineering and math) has been featured in recent years as a rewarding basket of opportune fields, not all STEM options are the same. "Engineering majors are nearly all high-paying. So are most computer and math majors, and math-heavy sciences like astrophysics. But many sciences, particularly the life sciences, pay below the overall median for recent college graduates."

Casselman looks at unemployment data too, and concludes that "...employers increasingly prefer applicants with bachelor's degrees even for jobs that don't traditionally require them. Nearly two-thirds of job postings for executive assistants now demand a bachelor's degree, even though only about one-fifth of people currently employed in the field have one. As a result, the unemployment rate for young college graduates is 5.8%, compared to 9.8% for those with a high school diploma but no bachelor's degree."

On the topic of underemployment, which has been much in the news since the "Great Recession," Casselman finds that engineering majors are among the least likely to be underemployed, joined by majors in the education and natural science fields. Likewise, nurses are among the least likely to be stuck in jobs that don't require the level of education they achieved. Contrastingly, graduates of programs like cosmetology, hospitality management, and human resources often do find themselves in non-college jobs. Drama and theater arts majors find things nearly as tough, with more than 30% in underemployed jobs. Other artists and performers are also near the bottom in this category. As Casselman puts it: "The stereotype of starving artists working in coffee shops has more than a bit of truth to it."

Another report that speaks to the question of which majors do best comes from Brad Hershbein and Melissa Kearney at the Hamilton Project. Entitled "Major Decisions: What Graduates Earn Over Their Lifetimes" (2014), this report draws on data from the Census Bureau's American Community Survey, and examines earnings for approximately 80 majors, looking at both annual earnings and cumulative lifetime earnings.

The report finds that median earnings of bachelor's degree graduates are higher than median earnings of high school graduates for all 80 majors studied. This is true at career entry, mid-career, and end of career. Median earnings of bachelor's degree graduates are at least as high as median earnings for associate's degree holders—again, throughout their career—for 76 out of 80 majors; the exceptions are early childhood education, elementary education, home economics, and social work.

Hershbein and Kearney also find that majors that emphasize quantitative skills tend to have graduates with the highest lifetime earnings. The highest-earning majors are those in engineering fields, computer science, operations and logistics, physics, economics, and finance. Majors that train students to work with children or provide counseling services tend to have graduates with the lowest earnings, such as early childhood education, family sciences (home economics), theology, fine arts, social work, and elementary education.

So, returning to the question I started with in this section, does the choice of major matter in terms of future earnings? Big time. Of course future earnings aren't the only criterion to consider. There may be others that are more important. We'll come to that topic in a bit.

Does It Matter *Where* You Go To College?

Hopefully by now I've made the point that college matters a lot, and that in general the more education you get the better you'll do financially, including not only at the bachelor's degree level but even above that. But this still leaves open the question of how much it matters *where* you go to college. Does getting into an elite college put you in a whole different realm than getting into simply a good one? The intense competition to get into one of the eight Ivy League schools, or the seven "Sisters," or comparable west coast elites like Stanford and Cal Tech and Berkeley, makes the headlines every spring when the latest admission rates are published.

There have been a number of studies that have looked at this question. In a piece published in *The Atlantic* May 17th, 2012, entitled "Does It Matter Where You Go To College?", Jordan Weissman concludes that it does matter. He grouped colleges into several categories and looked at wages of graduates six years after graduation. He made comparisons with "bottom-ranked public institutions", and found that graduates of "top private" colleges had a 39% earnings advantage in this comparison. Those from "top public" schools came next with a 26% advantage, followed by "middle private" and "middle public" colleges at 10% and 6% respectively. The bottom-ranked private schools showed a 15%

disadvantage. One issue in this study was that Weissman looked only at graduates, not all attendees. Since top schools typically have higher graduation rates, this may have biased the earnings findings in their favor.

A related study was done by Alan Kreuger of Princeton University and Stacy Berg Dale of the Andrew Mellon Foundation, published in 2000 by the National Bureau of Economic Research. They came to the somewhat curious conclusion it mattered less where you actually *attended* college than where you applied. These two researchers matched students who had been accepted by highly selective colleges, then compared those who chose to attend there with their counterparts who also got in but chose a "moderately selective" alternative instead. They found that these academic "siblings" ended up making "...just about the same wages after college regardless of how choosy their school was." Their conclusion: "If you were smart enough to get into Yale, or even take a shot at it, you were probably smart enough to earn like a Yale grad."

In a similar vein, in a piece entitled "It Doesn't Matter Where You Go to College" published in *Time* (April 10, 2014), Michael Bernick argues that attending an elite school won't make much difference in terms of your employment future. He cites the above Dale and Krueger study, but adds that a larger follow-up study released in 2011 that incorporated data from 19,000 graduates provides even stronger evidence that "...whether you went to Penn or Penn State, Williams College or Miami University of Ohio, job outcomes were unaffected in terms of earnings." What is important? "...what you will do, at college and in life, to keep improving your skills, to develop your character, to remain persistent."

So the evidence is a bit mixed on this count, but the weight of the argument indicates that it isn't crucial to get into a top-flight college to wind up doing well. More recent books have come to similar conclusions, one of them by Frank Bruni, an Op Ed columnist for the *New York Times*. Entitled "Where You Go Is Not Who You'll Be: An Antidote to the College Admissions Mania" (2015, Hachette Book Group), he points out that your chances of admission at highly selective colleges are less than 10% to begin with, and lower than that if you're not a legacy. He concludes that more important than getting into such a school, by far, in his many years of studying successful graduates, is that college is mostly what you make of it, and that "...qualities like resilience, perseverance, determination and cleverness aren't the province of any one echelon of school."

Will a College Degree Level the Playing Field for First Timers?

Another question in this college-going debate is whether college is really going to make a lifetime difference for young people who are the first in their families to achieve this goal. I've been discussing averages; what about this subset of students? What are the long-term effects of completing college for our "first in their family" kids compared with classmates who came from higher socioeconomic status backgrounds?

Here the data are fairly clear: once first-timers finish college, they do just as well as everyone else in most respects that have been studied. To summarize this in a nutshell: Among students who earn college degrees, occupational types, incomes, and many cognitive and non-cognitive skills are largely equivalent regardless of a family history of attending college.

To be precise, Susan Choy's work at the National Center for Education Statistics showed that one year after college graduation, 19.4% of students whose parents did *not* attend college were managers, 25.4% were professionals, and 8.3% worked in technical fields. For youth *with* college-educated parents, these percentages were 19.0%, 26.6%, and 8.0%, respectively. In short, essentially identical outcomes. A four-year college degree catapults first-generation college students into a new level of career opportunity, equivalent to peers whose parents did attend college.

Choy also showed that when you look at salaries three years after college graduation, gender, GPA, major, and college institution all shaped salaries, but parents' education did not, indicating that once you complete college your salary is not dependent on your parents' educational achievement.

Additionally, analyzing a sample of students from a diverse range of colleges across the nation through their third year of enrollment, Ernest Pascarella and colleagues (2004) found no meaningful differences in cognitive and non-cognitive development between first-generation students and their peers. It appears that college completion represents a major stride towards leveling the playing field regardless of parental education.

Let me address an often-cited concern here. Some have argued that the cognitive and non-cognitive similarities found among college graduates, regardless of parental education, may have mostly to do with the kinds of youth who are able to make the jump to college (what researchers call "social selection"). That is, maybe it isn't going to college that makes the difference, but the abilities of the young people who manage to rise above their parents' educational achievements. Put simply, maybe these kids are just smarter.

As I've explained, to gauge the effect of family relationships on educational attainment *across* abilities, *I controlled for aptitude in every analysis presented in this book.* That is, I looked at the effect of family relationships on youth's college going, holding aptitude constant. And the benefits hold across the full range of student aptitudes.

However, I need to be fair in acknowledging certain cautions. First-generation college graduates are less likely to attend graduate school, may lean toward studying different fields than peers who are following in their parents' footsteps, and on average can rely on less of a family financial safety net after college than peers who replicate their parents' college attainment. So a few discrepancies do remain even for college graduates.

Further, those who are successful do have to overcome many disadvantages. Youth from less-educated families approach the playing field with different odds of educational success. They may lack any or all of the following:

- Financial resources
- Information about when and how to plan for college
- Information about what college is like and what it takes to succeed
- Family support in the form of shared time and shared enthusiasm for their interests
- Parental encouragement in the form of conversations

about education and career goals and plans for achieving them

A deficit in any of these areas can pose serious barriers. Even among high-achieving high school students, presumably those with high level skills, having college-educated parents makes a difference.

So don't let me create the impression that being the first in your family to go to college is easy, even if you're unusually able. Rather, the point is that for those who overcome the barriers, a college degree can dramatically improve the imbalance. That's the bottom line. While there is no way to pretend the path upward is an easy one, for those who make it through this gauntlet the future is bright. The American Dream of upward mobility is real.

Is It Just About Money? Are There Other Outcomes Worth Considering?

Our discussions to this point have primarily looked at the financial differences between going to college and not doing so. As I've demonstrated, the data are pretty convincing: in most cases, going to college is definitely worth it. Lifetime earnings correlate highly with educational levels. If a college education were valuable in the past, it's even more valuable today. Majors matter, but in virtually every field, a bachelor's degree improves one's earnings, and a higher degree does so even more. It doesn't matter dramatically where you go to college; what matters most is that you do. And if you follow this advice and earn a bachelor's degree, and happen to be a young person from a family with no history of college going, this will pretty much level the playing field for you in terms of skills and future earnings in your chosen field.

But what if future earnings aren't the biggest concern? What about a young person who is a budding painter, or dancer, or playwright, or comedian, or musician, or philosopher, or any of a dozen other fields not associated with high earnings for any but a few. Does college matter then? Are there outcomes other than financial ones that argue for going to college?

There have been a number of studies looking into this question. While they vary in the details, they have a number of findings in common. For example, a study by Sandy Baum and Jennifer Ma entitled "Education pays: The benefits of higher education for individuals and society" (2010) found the following:

> Higher job quality. Money is one thing; job benefits are something else. The two may be related, but they're not identical. Adults 25 and over with a college degree, on average, find themselves in more rewarding jobs with better benefits (e.g., health insurance, paid sick and vacation leave, retirement assistance). In fact, sometimes the benefits associated with higher-level employment are worth more than the salary differences.
>
> More satisfying work. On average, college-educated adults find their work more satisfying. They usually have more options to choose among in selecting a job, and thus can select one closer to their likings. They also often get more positive feedback from the people they're working with, including their clients.
>
> Better health. College-educated adults smoke less, exercise more, and enjoy generally better health. For example, a study using 2005 data found that 9% of adults 25 and over with a bachelor's degree smoked compared to 26% of those with just a high school diploma. Sixty-two percent exercised vigorously at least once per week, compared with 31% of high school grads.
>
> More civic involvement. More adults with bachelor's degrees volunteer, at over a two-to-one ratio, and more give blood. More also vote: 76% of bachelor's educated adults aged 25-44 in this study voted in the 2004 election, compared with 49% of high school graduates.

Another report, "The Nonfinancial Benefits of Higher Education for Individuals and Society," published by Susan Madsen (2012), drew on several sources. Her findings covered some of the same ground, but added others:

> Well-Being. Closely aligned with the findings regarding better health above, adults with bachelor's degrees, compared with those with only a high school diploma, live longer, exercise more, are less obese, smoke less, and have healthier diets, lower rates of alcohol abuse, and lower cholesterol levels. They also

have fewer low-birth weight babies, spend more time reading to their children, and their children participate in more extracurricular activities.

Civic life, social skills, tolerance, happiness. Like the previous report, this one found higher rates of voting, blood donations, and volunteer activities among college-educated adults. It also found lower rates of crime, suicide, poverty, and use of Medicaid and food stamps. It found higher levels of self-esteem, better interpersonal skills, better analytical and quantitative skills, more openness to diversity and racial understanding, and more reflective reasoned judgments. And college-educated respondents were happier, more resilient, and less depressed.

That's quite a list. While not all these findings are necessarily intuitive, with a little reflection they make a lot of sense. College brings young people into contact with well-educated professors, upper classmen, and often graduate students, who usually have well-developed communication and quantitative skills. College students are asked to discuss issues and write papers in many of their classes, gaining stronger communication skills. They will probably brush shoulders with a wider range of students compared to high school, where everyone likely came from a nearby neighborhood. They will gain a tolerance for differences in upbringings, attitudes, and views. They will be around more research and reports, and will be exposed to what we collectively know in many fields on many topics. And they will have a few more years to learn who they are and how their traits and interests might match the wide range of possible careers available to them. For these reasons, none of which pertain directly to finances, college is typically a rewarding experience.

Chapter 3

Who Goes to College?

The stage is set. The previous chapter shows that college is a valuable investment by *many* measures, including income and quality of life. It's time to begin looking at some original research—research that is being published for the first time in these pages.

Let me offer one caution before I begin: this chapter is full of data, figures, correlations, and comparisons. If wading through some fairly dense statistical information about who attends college doesn't sound like your cup of tea, please feel free to skip to Chapter 4, where I begin to talk about the value of *family relationships* for children's educational achievements in more depth.

Digging into the numbers, let's look first at the most basic data I have, which provide a picture of who goes how far in their educational journey by their mid-twenties. Figure 1 presents a picture of the National Longitudinal Survey of Youth (NLSY97) across the spectrum of educational levels achieved. To understand Figure 1 clearly, let me provide two brief explanations.

First, these percentages represent the *highest level* of schooling completed in each case. While this seems obvious, the reason to mention it is that those young people with, say, a graduate degree have also attained a bachelor's degree (though they're not counted among the 19 % whose *highest* attainment is a bachelor's degree). Likewise, those with some college have most likely completed high school or a GED, but they're not counted among the proportion of kids whose *highest* attainment is high school or a GED. Second, these numbers represent "weighted distributions." Put simply, this means that the data presented should match the achievements of youth across America.

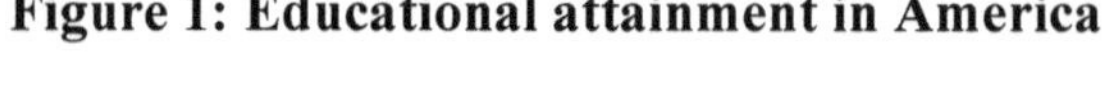

Figure 1: Educational attainment in America

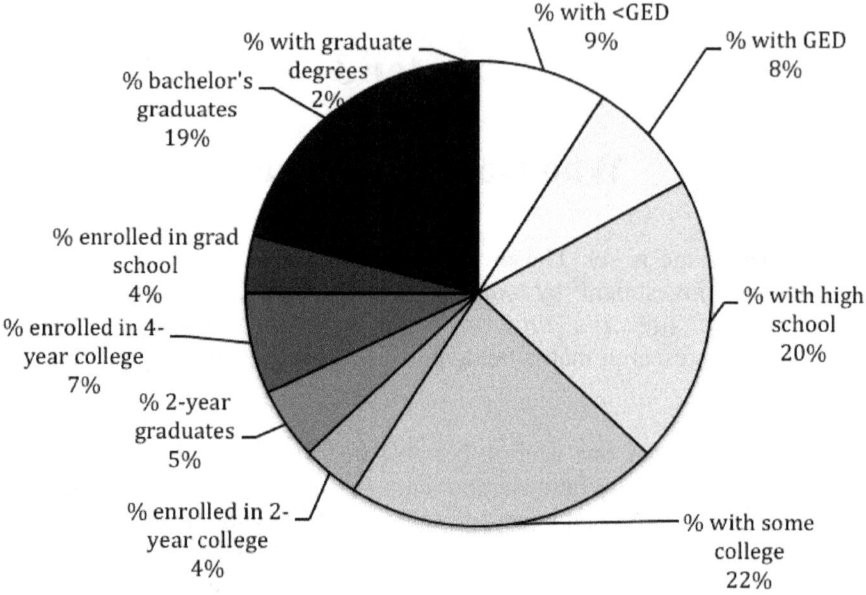

The most common highest attainments are:

- A high school degree (20%)
- Some college experience but no degree (22%)
- A bachelor's degree (19%)

In short, by their early to mid-twenties about one-fifth of American young people follows each of these paths.

Turning to the least common attainments, by their early to mid-twenties few had earned a graduate degree (2%) or were enrolled in graduate school (4%). The chart also highlights that traditional-age college going is far more common than doing so later: continuing enrollment beyond the mid-twenties in a two-year college is relatively rare (4%), as is continuing enrollment in a four-year college (7%).

Whose kids go to college? Parent education and family income

Now let's look at how these educational paths correlate with parent education and family income in Figures 2 and 3. These illustrate the broad trends we're all familiar with. Young people tend to achieve higher levels of education if their parents are more highly educated and/or their families have higher incomes. Contrastingly, they tend to achieve less education if their parents are less educated and/or their families have lower incomes. Note that in Figures 2 and 3, lighter-colored segments represent lower educational attainments, while darker segments represent higher attainments, and the attainments of children with more educated and higher income parents show up as increasingly darker.

Taking a close look at Figure 2, youth are *most* likely to follow the same educational path as their parents. Among those whose parents dropped out of high school, relatively few have achieved higher educations. But nearly a third of those with bachelor's-educated parents have earned bachelor's degrees, another near-fifth are enrolled in either four-year college or graduate school, and one in twenty-five has already earned a graduate degree. This underscores why first-generation college going is so impressive.

Looking at educational attainment by family income, shown in Figure 3, the patterns mirror those seen by parents' level of schooling in Figure 2. Youth from the two lowest income brackets are most likely to complete their educations with high school, those from the second-highest income-quartile are most likely to have some college education, and those from the highest income-quartile are most likely to earn bachelor's degrees. In short, there is a strong association between family income and educational achievement.

Figure 2: Educational attainment among kids whose parents achieved less than high school, high school, some college, and bachelor's educations

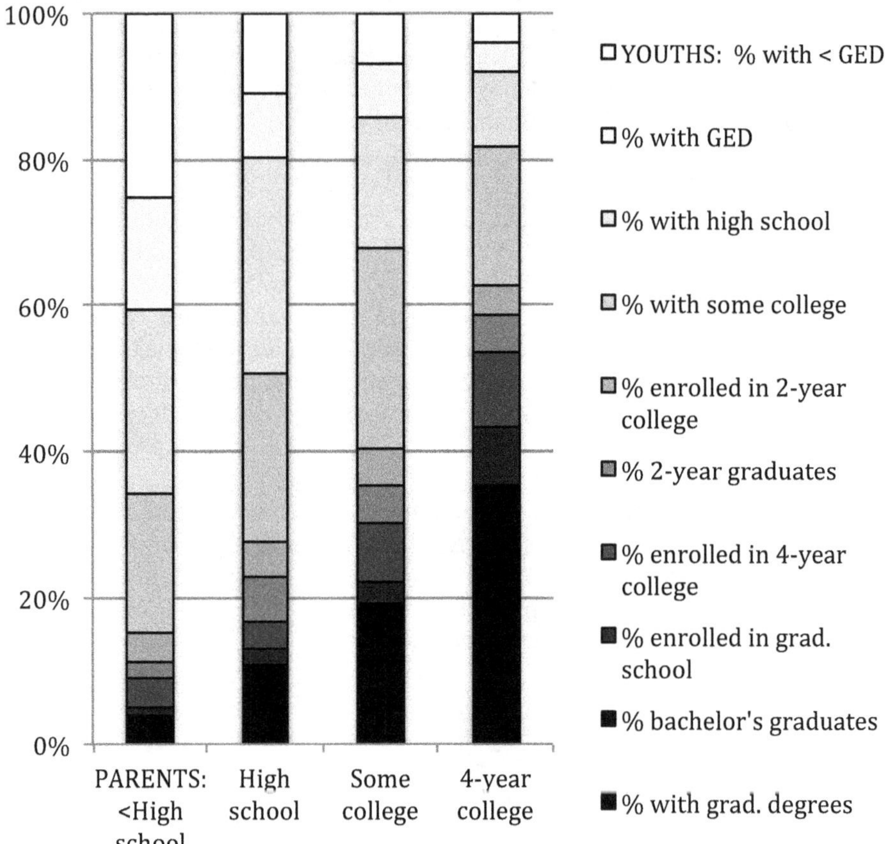

Figure 3: Educational attainment among quartiles of family income

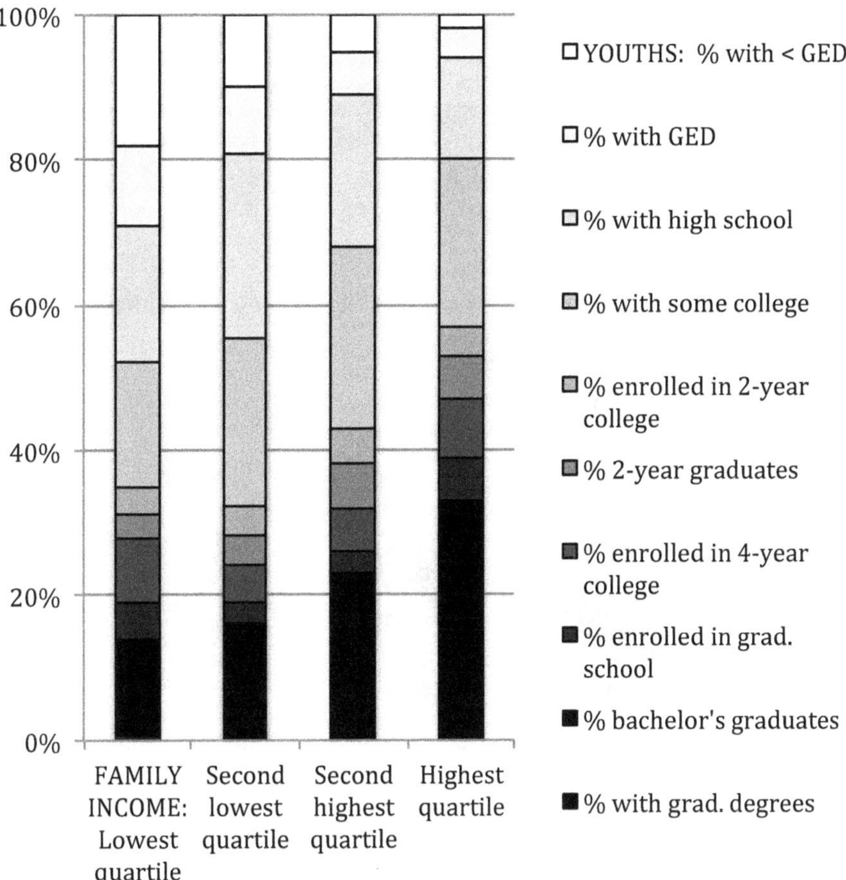

What about gender and race?

Now let's look at differences associated with gender and race/ethnicity, beginning with gender in Figure 4. Historically, males have had higher educational achievements than females. Indeed, many colleges began as all-male institutions and only started admitting women somewhere along the way. But this gender balance has been shifting, and today females tend to predominate in higher education. Figure 4 shows that in 2007, while a minority (41%) of students with no college experience were female, a slight majority (52%) of those with some college were female, as were even more (56%) of students with four years of college. Conversely, while 59% of no-college students were male, 48% of some-college students were male, as were just 44% of four-year college students.

Figure 4: Gender of students who reach no college, some college, and four-year college

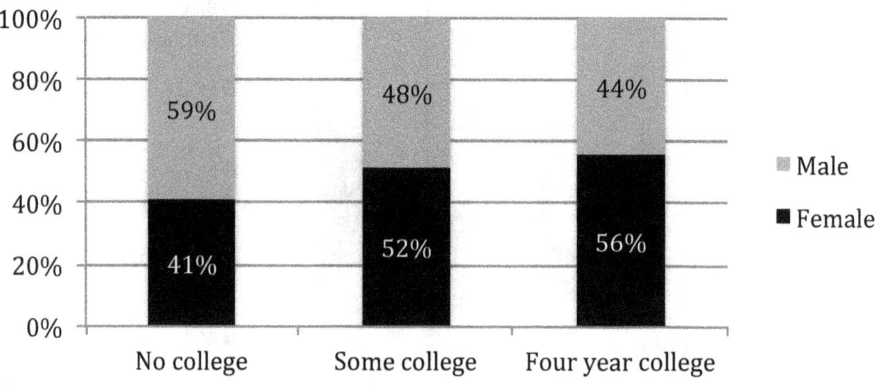

This trend is one that has continued, including at higher levels of education. Here's a brief summary of the picture in 2013, from the President of the California State Board of Education, who is also a professor at Stanford University, Dr. Michael Kirst:

> According to data from the Department of Education on college degrees by gender, the US college degree gap favoring women started back in 1978, when for the first time ever, more women than men earned Associate's degrees. Five years later, in 1982, women earned more bachelor's

> degrees than men for the first time, and women have increased their share of bachelor's degrees in every year since then. In another five years, by 1987, women earned the majority of master's degrees for the first time. Finally, within another decade, more women than men earned doctor's degrees by 2006, and female domination of college degrees at every level was complete. For the current graduating class of 2013, the Department of Education estimates that women will earn 61.6% of all associate's degrees this year, 56.7% of all bachelor's degrees, 59.9% of all master's degrees, and 51.6% of all doctor's degrees. Overall, 140 women will graduate with a college degree at some level this year for every 100 men (in an article from *AEI Ideas* as summarized by the Carnegie Foundation).

Next let's look at race/ethnicity. In Figure 5, the bars show the percentage of no-college, some-college, and four-year college students who are non-Hispanic White, Asian/ American Indian, Black and Hispanic. For example, Figure 5 shows that while 61% of no-college students are White, 64% of some-college students and 76% of four-year college students are White. In contrast, 20% of no-college students are Black, as are 18% of some-college students, and just 9% of four-year college students.

Figure 5: Race/ethnicity of students who reach no college, some college, and four-year college

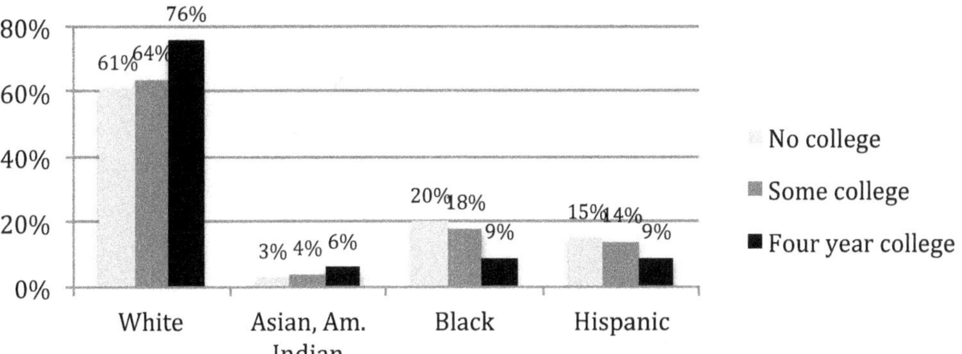

All of the White percentages are relatively high because a high percentage of the population is White. That's not what's interesting in Figure 5. What's interesting is the difference between no-college, some-college, and four-year college percentages *within each race/ethnicity*. Whites are most highly represented among four-year college students and least represented among no-college students. The same is true for Asians/American Indians. But Blacks are most highly represented among no-college students and least represented among four-year college students, as are Hispanics. So the balance tips in opposite directions for Whites and Asians/American Indians on the one hand, who are more often highly educated, compared to Blacks and Hispanics on the other, who are less likely to reach four-year college.

Intergenerational attainment

Now let's take a look at these same relationships in a way that highlights *intergenerational* educational paths. To be clear about each of the intergenerational paths I talk about, I use the term "legacy" to describe youth who follow in their parents' footsteps, including when both parents and children attend four-year college ("bachelor's legacies"), when both parents and children attend some college ("some-college legacies"), and when both parents and children do not attend college ("no-college legacies").

Somewhat more obviously, I use the term "first-generation bachelor's" to describe students who become the first in their family to attend four-year college, and "downwardly mobile bachelor's" for students who fall short of their parents' bachelor's education. Somewhat tediously (but I haven't been able to land on better language), I refer to "first-generation some-college students" for those who become the first in their family to attend any college, and "downwardly-mobile some-college students" for those who fall short of their parents' achievement of some-college education.

Beginning with family income, see Figure 6. Because family income is correlated to parent education, a minority of first-generation students comes from families with above-average family incomes. That is, while 71% of bachelor's legacies have above-average family incomes, only 41% of no-college legacies do.

There are two ways to understand the family income patterns presented in Figure 6. The first is that first-generation students, on average, are at an economic disadvantage compared to their college-legacy peers, particularly in the case of bachelors-level achievements. This underscores how impressive first-generation college going is, as it is generally achieved with limited family financial resources. The second is that first-generation students do have a slight economic advantage over their no-college legacy peers. This highlights the association between access to financial resources and educational attainment. It also underscores the importance of examining the role of family relationships in educational mobility across *all* levels of income.

Figure 6: Percent of students with above-average family incomes who follow each intergenerational educational path

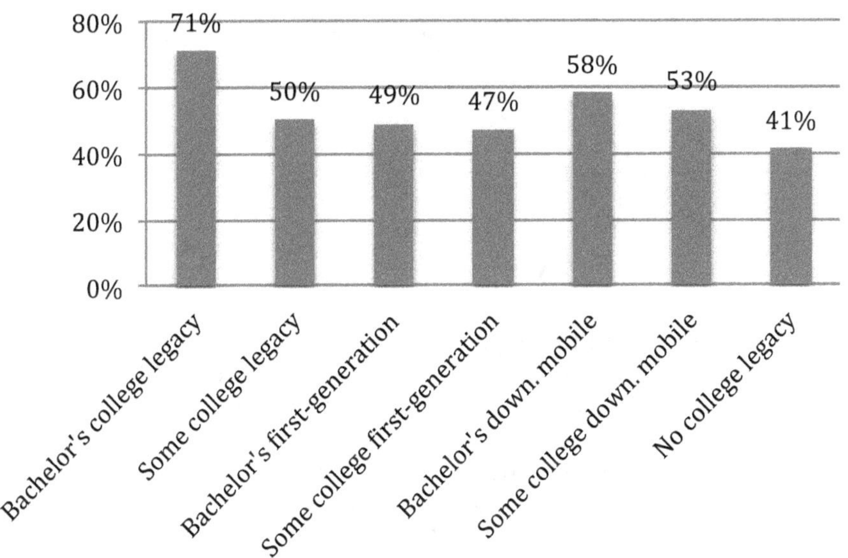

Turning to gender in Figure 7, it is striking that the higher-attainment trajectories (the four left-most bars) are all dominated by women, while men dominate the three downward mobility bars. Again, this matches other recent research which finds that women have made substantial educational gains over the past few decades. In fact, first-generation college students are half-again as likely to be female as male.

Figure 7: Percent of female and male students who follow each intergenerational educational path

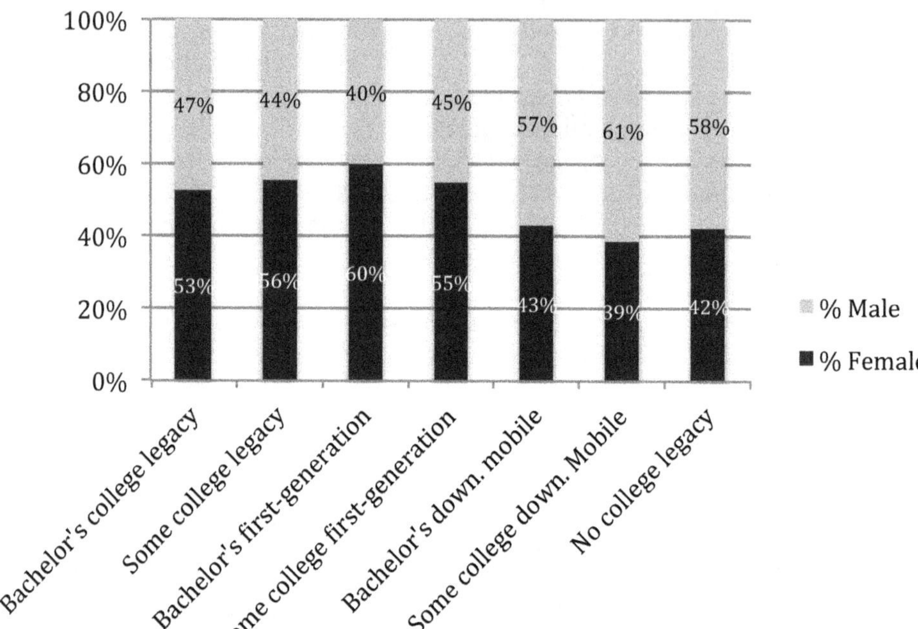

Next let's turn to the percentage of each attainment group that falls into each race/ethnicity, as illustrated in Figure 8. A few things stand out here. First, White youth comprise four of every five (80%) bachelor's legacies, and 71% of some-college legacies (compared to a two-thirds representation in the overall sample). Contrastingly, they constitute only 56% of no-college legacies. These are the young people with the greatest educational advantages. However, they also comprise an average number of downwardly mobile bachelor's, and a higher than average some-college downwardly mobile group. In short, they're losing ground.

In turn, first-generation some-college students are more likely to be Black or Hispanic: 23% of Black youth fall into this category (compared to their 16% representation in the overall sample), as do 19% of Hispanic kids (compared to their 13% representation in the overall sample). This is most easily visualized with the some-college first-generation bars (in solid gray) standing tall in Figure 8.

These two groups aren't yet earning bachelor's degrees in higher numbers, but they are getting close, and are more apt to be first-generation college attenders than their proportion of the sample would predict. There is no real surprise here; both of these findings replicate what previous studies have found.

Figure 8: Race/ethnicity of students who follow each intergenerational educational path

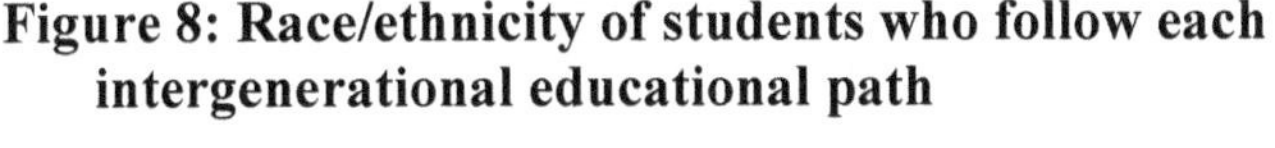

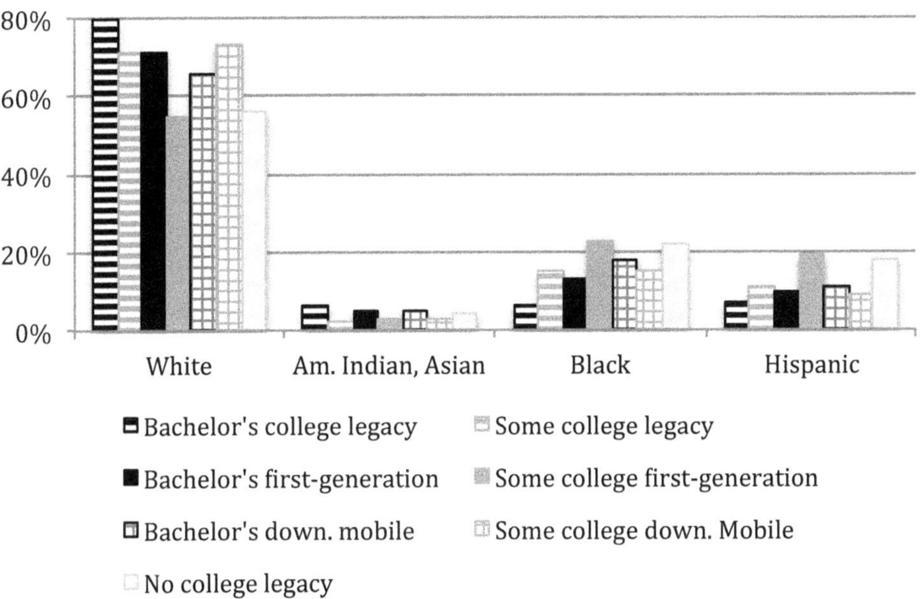

Trends in college going—and the challenge of being a first-generation student

The above figures and discussion provide a picture of demographic disparities in college going. Other research contributes to an understanding of just how challenging it is to become a first-generation college student. Looking back over the past several decades, Michael Hout, a professor at U.C. Berkeley, documented (2008) that college graduation increased by about half a percentage point per year among those entering college from 1955-1969, and by a full percentage point for those who entered college from 1970-1984. However, this expansion slowed for youth who entered college from 1985-1999, and college going has only risen by half a percentage point per year since.

Looking inside these numbers, Victor Saenz and colleagues at the Higher Education Research Institute (2007) showed that today's first-generation college students are more likely to be Hispanic, foreign-born, have attended rural or small-town high schools, come from households in which English is not the primary language, and have lower-than-average college-goers' SAT scores. In general they are at a disadvantage compared with their college peers in terms of educational preparation and expectations, family income and support, and knowledge about college costs and application procedures, as Ernest Pascarrela (2004) and colleague Patrick Terenzini (1998), Susan Choy (2001), and Laura Horn and Anne-Marie Nunez (2000) have all documented.

Further, high school supports do not appear to make up for a lack of college-assistance at home. For example, Susan Choy's National Center for Education Statistics report showed that while a third of college-qualified high school graduates report that their high school helped them in preparing an admissions essay, and over half report help of some sort in completing college applications, there are no significant differences in the amount of help provided students based on parents' levels of schooling. Thus high schools don't appear to be compensating for a lack of resources at home (see also Horn and Nunez 2000).

Even once enrolled, first-generation college students confront cultural, social, and academic challenges. Ernest Pascarrela and colleagues (2004) found that they are more likely to leave college after a single year and less likely to be enrolled or earn a bachelor's degree after five years. Again, Saenz and colleagues showed that they more often work towards the end of high school and during college, and are twice as likely to report major concerns about financing college compared with their college-legacy peers.

Likewise, Robert Bozick (2007) revealed that students who live in their family home to save money during the first year of college, and those who work more than twenty hours a week, more often leave school during their first year than those who live on campus and work less than this. Lower socioeconomic status students also experience more frequent interruptions like school transfers and breaks, as Sara Goldrick-Rab demonstrated (2006). And Terry

Ishitani (2003) found the rates of attrition to be 71% higher among first-generation students when compared with children of two-college-educated parents, even when controlling for race, gender, high school GPA, and family income.

First-generation college students also take longer on average to finish college. In this study, they were twice as likely as college-legacy students to be enrolled in four-year college at the end of my analyses. That is, while about four percent of my sample was comprised of first-generation students who were still enrolled, only about two percent of the sample was comprised of college-legacy students still enrolled.

Further, at least a few challenges faced by first-generation students remain after college completion. For example, research from the National Center for Education Statistics (Choy 2001) showed that first-generation students are less likely to enroll in graduate school than their peers, and to have a family financial "safety net", than those from affluent families, should they struggle in establishing their careers.

All these comparisons illustrate the influences of family socioeconomic status (SES) on youth's college going and completion. In short, youth who come from families with no history of college going face a gauntlet of daunting challenges. These comparisons illustrate just how demanding overcoming these challenges is for such youth. First-generation college attendance and completion represent huge achievements.

Where does this leave us?

That's a lot of information to absorb. But you've now waded through the densest of the data. And this will help you appreciate what much of this book is about: Namely, how do those first-time college goers do it? Read on.

In their own words:
How I became a first-generation college student
from a Hispanic female from the West

Me and my parents, we all knew I wanted to go to college, I needed to go to college. My Mom, she works at a warehouse. Every once in a while she'd just be like, "Just keep working hard so you don't have to work with me, or where your Dad works. So you don't have to work in the warehouse or the orchard." That definitely served as a daily reminder. They were definitely very supportive.

I wanted to be a nurse, and so that was our main conversation. I'd say "I'm staying involved in such-and-such activity because I'm going to be applying to college," or "I'm applying to scholarships now," or "This is what I'm going to be doing in this club to give me points for my resume," so they would understand why I was doing it. They were very supportive. They'd say, "Oh that's good. I'm really happy for you. Keep it up. Get good grades." You know like, "Please have a better life than us," basically.

I think as a migrant, that's definitely been a huge thing in making me drive to do something, strive for something better. It was my parents (she begins to cry). I think it was my parents that got me here. I think it was just seeing them work so hard. I think, consciously or subconsciously, it just really motivated me. I just felt very grateful and I wanted to do something for me but also for them in a sense. I wanted all their support for me to be worth it for them. And for me that was the biggest thing. I think that was the reason I went to college.

Chapter 4

Social Capital—The Lynchpin

Let's take a moment to revisit the overarching ideas behind this study. In James Coleman's groundbreaking work of the last century, he wrote specifically about the role of families in children's educational development, arguing that families influence children by providing three fundamental resources: (1) human capital, typically measured by parent education; (2) financial capital, generally measured by family income; and (3) social capital, captured in family interactions. This chapter will summarize the research done previously that pertains to this theory.

Parent education and family income—commonly referred to as "socioeconomic status" or "SES"— tend to go hand-in-hand as two of the strongest and most consistent predictors of children's educational attainment, even when you take into account a whole host of other characteristics. To illustrate this relationship, let's look at our topic here, college enrollment, and what makes it happen. The National Center for Education Statistics' impressive study on first-generation college students speaks to this (Choy 2001). It describes how college enrollment is the product of several sequential steps:

- Wanting to attend college
- Completing academic prerequisites
- Taking the SAT or ACT
- Completing applications and gaining acceptance
- Negotiating financial and other arrangements

For each step, youth with college-educated parents make better progress. And while about two-thirds of high school graduates from bachelor's-educated families ultimately enroll in a four-year college, just over a third from some-college educated families do, and just over a fifth of those from high school or less educated families do.

Similarly, many researchers in this arena have pointed out that families with the least educated parents and lowest incomes are also least likely to know about the road to college, the price of college, and how to succeed in college. Despite this, Gary Sandefur and colleagues (2006) demonstrated that the effects of parent education and family income on children's attainment are sometimes rivaled by the effects of social capital—which brings me back to Coleman's third pillar of family influence. Let's get into some specifics.

During the K-12 years one of the strongest predictors of academic success is the family environment, including parental encouragement and aspirations (see McCarron and Inkelas 2006, Bandura et al. 1996, Sewell & Hauser 1980). Sara McLanahan and Gary Sandefur (1994) showed that children from families with both parents present, in which there are on average more parent-hours to go around, are dramatically less likely to drop out of school. Even the physical environment parents create can influence educational attainment, as Rachel Dunifon and colleagues (2001) showed: children raised in clean, organized homes have higher educational attainment twenty-five years later, even when controlling for parents' education, cognitive skills, and other relevant variables. This research may provide clues about what parents can do to encourage college going.

Many more studies speak to the difference families can make. For example, when parents know their children's friends' parents, their children have higher achievement in math and are less likely to drop out of school (Carbonaro 1998). Likewise, parent-child discussions, and parental monitoring and support, are associated with fewer behavioral problems and lower likelihood of school dropout. These two factors alone bear a stronger association to these outcomes than do cognitive measures (McNeal 1999). Frequent family conversations about school predict children's college going, as do parental expectations for children to earn bachelor's degrees and parent involvement in children's schools (Sandefur, Meier, and Campbell 2005).

College-educated families are more likely to embody these kinds of relationships than are less-educated families. For example, Susan Choy's report showed that 61% of high school graduates with bachelor's-educated parents frequently discussed postsecondary plans as a family during their senior year of high school. In contrast, only 42% of those whose parents did not attend college did so. Likewise, while 82% of students with bachelor's-educated parents visited a postsecondary institution as a family, only 61% of those whose parents did not attend college did so.

Here's one more: Laura Horn and Anne-Marie Nunez (2000) showed that college-educated parents are substantially more likely to encourage their children to take challenging courses in high school. Competitive colleges almost always look at a student's high school course taking patterns, where the difficulty of courses taken can be more important than their grades, at least assuming the grades are okay. This kind of knowledge—and knowing about Advanced Placement (AP) and honors courses, which are typically more academically rigorous and require more homework, but which also support advanced learning and help prepare students for college-level academics—provides an edge for students in the know.

Another body of literature, founded by Pierre Bourdieu (1973), examines how educated families are more likely to endow their children with cultural characteristics (termed "cultural capital") that communicate to teachers and other influential adults, " I belong in educated circles." This can include things like speaking styles, fashion preferences, and extracurricular interests. For example, picture a neatly dressed student describing her appreciation for fine arts with careful enunciation. This student is saying, "I'm headed for higher education" just by the way she presents herself. These kinds of characteristics often do not relate directly to educational success, but they can be seen as signals that students are bound for success. Highly educated parents are more likely to possess preferences and prefer styles that signal status, so these kinds of characteristics are more likely to be passed down through shared time and strong relationships within higher SES families. This is one more reason why social capital (i.e., shared time and strong relationships) within high SES families helps children succeed.

All of this illustrates how human, financial, and social capital are intertwined: higher parent credentials qualify parents for jobs with higher incomes, and more highly-educated families tend to share more of the interactions and dynamics found valuable for educational achievement. Human, financial, and social capital tend to come as a bundle.

However, their intertwining influences *can* pull in different directions. For example, if income comes at the cost of shared time, children's educational attainment may suffer. Martha Hill and Greg Duncan (1987) showed that having a full-time employed mother—which increases financial capital but decreases opportunities for interaction—significantly *reduced* their sons' educational attainment. So while income is generally beneficial for educational attainment, *if* it comes at the cost of shared family time, it may reduce educational attainment.

John Shea (2000) found that differences in income due essentially to luck (such as involuntary job loss from a plant closing, or a job's union status) generally have a minor impact on children's educations. Likewise, changes in income due to factors aside from parents' qualifications and achievements seem to have little effect on children's attainment, supporting the idea that income per se is not the most powerful lever on children's achievements (see Blau 1999, Duflo 1999, and Mayer 1997).

In fact, Karl White (1982) conducted a meta-analysis that examined over one hundred studies, and found that family interactions were substantially more highly correlated with academic achievement than was SES. What kinds of family interactions? Here are some typical examples of shared activities, communications, and circumstances within a family:

- Family church attendance
- Family cultural activities
- Parent attitudes toward education
- Parent attitudes toward children's aspirations
- Academic guidance from parents
- The quality of language used at home
- The presence of reading materials in the home
- The tone and frequency of family conversations

All of these are examples of valuable family social capital, and they have been found to bear a stronger correlation to academic achievement than variables of socioeconomic status.

Other research tells even more about how parenting styles can affect children's achievements. The phrases "concerted cultivation" and "natural growth" come into play here. In her groundbreaking study, Annette Lareau (2002) found that higher SES parents typically exercise "concerted cultivation." This means they organize their children's leisure time to foster attitudes and behaviors likely to open future opportunities for them. They also coach them in how to relate to other adults. For example, youth are encouraged to become involved in extracurricular activities, they are often enrolled in after-school lessons and encouraged to join teams, are discouraged from watching TV, and are taught reasoning skills and encouraged to talk with their teachers and coaches.

In contrast, lower SES parents more often practice "natural growth." This means they provide a safe, loving environment in which children can thrive, but less guidance and direction concerning what kinds of activities to engage in. For example, such youth are often left to their own devices to fill leisure time, which generally results in more time spent playing in the neighborhood and with extended family members. In addition, such parents tend to give their children more directives (e.g., "It's time to clean up, because I said so"), rather than encouraging them to practice and develop their own reasoning.

"Concerted cultivation" and "natural growth" represent two varieties of family interactions that appear to prepare children for different educational trajectories. Note again, these are not behaviors for the most part limited by financial considerations or past education. Rather they are options any family can choose from.

The literature on "family resilience" points to yet more such possibilities. This body of research has emphasized how families rebound from challenging events, overcoming hardships and avoiding pitfalls such as substance abuse and teenage pregnancy (for example, see Seccombe 2002, Gofen 2007, and Simon and colleagues 2005). It identifies the interaction styles and dynamics that allow families to thrive in the face of adversity. These characteristics include:

- Warmth, affection and emotional support for one another
- Family cohesion and commitment
- Reasonable and clear-cut expectations for children
- Family celebrations and traditions
- Predictable routines
- Spiritual connections
- Shared core values around financial management and use of leisure time

Less common is research investigating how families can rise above challenging situations and grow in positive ways. Rather than thinking of resilient characteristics just as strategies for responding to difficult situations or events, they can also be seen as a means for reaching new heights. For example, by definition the families of first-generation college students lack human capital; their parents didn't attend college. And most first-generation families face financial challenges. But none of the above examples require either of these. These resilient characteristics are all aspects of valuable family social capital, and they may well serve to support children's success against the odds.

In fact, some research has already shown that strong family relationships can be meaningful *specifically* for less advantaged families. Robert Crosnoe and colleagues (2002) found that disadvantaged parents who believed they could influence their children's trajectories were more actively engaged, more often helping adolescents to map out opportunities and manage their lives, and steering them into protective environments. Glen Elder and colleagues (1995) showed how even under economic strain, parents can facilitate their children's success by monitoring their whereabouts, enforcing curfews, suggesting role models, studying with them, fostering their interests, and taking advantage of special programs or classes.

Similarly, Jerry Trusty (1998) found that parent support and involvement in adolescents' academic and social lives—measured by whether parents attended school activities, helped with homework, engaged in entertainment outside of school, attended family functions, and took trips and vacations together—predicted educational expectations more strongly for low SES students than for their high SES counterparts. Further, he suggested that interventions aimed to improve parent-child communication, parental support, and parental attendance at school activities might be *especially* beneficial for low SES youth.

Strong family relationships also help explain why children from some low-SES Asian-American families surpass Whites' educational performance, as Kimberly Goyette and Yu Xie demonstrated (1999) in a study of educational expectations. Illustrating this, some years ago a school district noticed many Asian immigrant families were buying *two* of their children's required school textbooks. This seemed strange to teachers and administrators; when they looked into it, they learned it was so that those parents could study alongside their children so they could help them when needed (see Coleman 1987). These families were not highly educated—the parents didn't know the material their children were being taught—but still wanted to find a way to invest in their children's educational success.

More generally, a report from the Higher Education Research Institute (Saenz et al 2007) found that over the past fifteen years, college students from all backgrounds have increasingly reported parental encouragement as an important reason for attending college. In fact, first-generation college students' reports of parental encouragement more than doubled during this time, surpassing even college-educated parents' reported encouragement. This suggests that the American Dream of upward mobility may be more alive than ever.

In a similar vein, a qualitative study by Anat Gofen (2007) based on fifty in-depth, semi-structured interviews with first-generation college students found that first-generation students unanimously credited their educational success to specific family interactions and dynamics. This research identified common themes in young people's discussions of their educational success:

- Having long-term educational goals
- Parents' awareness of students' school experiences, such as their test schedules
- Daily homework routines
- Taking advantage of school choice or enrolling in private schools
- Buying books and computers despite economic

challenges
- Not requiring students' help around the house
- Discouraging early marriage (especially for girls)
- Widely expressing pride in students

Strong parent-child relationships were also important when measured through parental expressions of unconditional love, sacrifice, aspirations for children, and belief in their children's abilities. From the children's perspective, strong relationships were evident in their recognition of their parents' investment in them and sense of duty to fulfill their expectations. Family solidarity was expressed through shared dinners and meetings on a regular basis, and a sense that families give to each other and stick together. Lastly, respect for parents was indicated by children holding their parents in high regard and avoiding quarreling within the family.

Of course, families don't exist in a vacuum. They live in neighborhoods, interact with their communities, and spend time at schools and jobs that necessarily influence how they function. There are lots of examples:

The neighborhood. Is it safe? Where can kids and families share time together? Is there healthy food easily available? Are there adequate numbers of good jobs for local adults?

Communities. Are there groups of people the family spends time with, such as churches or clubs or close family friends? What kinds of relationships do these community members share? Are they supportive of kids' interests? Are they knowledgeable about how young people can achieve their goals?

Schools. Are they safe? Are teachers supportive of young people's aspirations and knowledgeable about how to achieve them? Are parents encouraged to get involved? Is there a school culture that supports studying and taking school seriously?

Jobs. Do parents' jobs pay enough to support a family? Do parents need to work two or three jobs to pay their bills? Do they include benefits? Are they flexible regarding employees meeting their family needs?

Families are nested in many environments that influence how they interact and what their children are exposed to. A colleague and I conducted a comprehensive literature review exploring how social contexts like neighborhoods and schools affect youth outcomes; if this topic is of interest, check out DeLuca and Dayton (2009).

This book focuses on the explicit role of *families*. This chapter has reviewed many studies suggesting the importance of strong family relationships in promoting educational achievement. In the coming chapters, drawing on my own study, I add a pattern of broad national statistical verification to this body of research, with a specific eye to intergenerational educational paths. That's the crux of this book. Next, Chapter 5 provides an overview of the precise parenting styles I examine, and Chapter 6 delves into the resulting statistical findings.

Chapter 5

Parenting Styles

I have now reviewed what past studies have shown about the importance of social capital, and more specifically, the impact of family relationships on educational outcomes. Now let me move to an explanation of my own research approach. To talk about family relationships more deeply, I categorize them into three dimensions: opportunity, tone, and substance.

As a starting point, there needs to be *opportunities* for interaction within a family. Without time together, meaningful interactions have no chance to emerge. Family structures affect opportunities for such interaction on a basic level. For example, having both parents present and fewer siblings involved increases the number of parent-hours available per child, at least in principle. Single-parent families, particularly those with more children, have a disadvantage in this regard. But other factors also play an important role. For example, shared family routines, such as dinners, hobbies, or celebrations all strengthen family bonds and provide occasions for meaningful conversations.

Second, in the context of shared family time, the *tone* of interactions matters. A family in which children feel supported and are monitored by parents is more likely to encourage planning and ambitions than one defined by cold or untrusting relationships or unengaged parents.

Third, the *substance* of what is shared within a family also makes a difference. Parents who talk with their children about educational and career aspirations and who are involved in their academic and social lives can help to focus children, steering them towards goals and keeping them attuned to those goals. This can happen even without a first-hand knowledge of what a given achievement is like, such as having attended college themselves, and without large financial resources to bolster such achievement.

In these ways, family relationships—social capital—can be understood as a critical resource for educational achievement, with or without the twin forces of high parent education and income.

Given the increasingly clear value of supportive family relationships for children's achievements, let's turn to the actual questions young people across the country were asked in the database I used. In research parlance these questions are the *independent variables*. We're interested in seeing which has an effect on the outcome we're studying—that is, our *dependent variable*, namely college going.

Opportunity

I use two variables to measure the first dimension, *opportunities* for family interaction:

- **Family structure:** *Are both parents present?* This is important because single-parent family structures can limit the time parents have to devote to children, restricting the extent to which parents may foster children's abilities and facilitate their success in school.

- **Siblings:** *How many children live in the household?* Increasing numbers of siblings typically dilute parents' attention to each child, again restricting their investment in each child's education. To be precise, I look at whether there are more than two siblings present.

These are approximate measures of how many opportunities there are for interaction in a family. There may be lots of parental contact with a single parent and/or several children, and if you fall into that category, these measures clearly would not capture opportunities for interaction within your family. If I were to design my own survey I would ask much more specific questions to assess opportunities for family interaction.

But the downside of designing my own survey would have been talking to many fewer families over much less time—I wouldn't have a decade of data for thousands of kids. That's the overwhelming strength of the National Longitudinal Survey of Youth (NLSY97). And the questions the NLSY97 asked to determine the tone and substance of family interactions are good, as you'll see in the coming pages. My approximations of opportunities for family interaction are in line with what others have written about the influence of the number of parents and children in the household on the number of hours each child gets with a parent—that is, the amount of opportunity a child has to interact with parents. This theme was also reflected in many of the conversations I had with first-generation college students.

In their own words:
Opportunities for first-generation family interaction
from a Hispanic female from the Midwest

My parents have always had a good relationship with each other. I was actually just thinking about this recently: Of my closest friends, who has good parent relationships? And I could think of one other person whose parents were together and happy. And so I don't really know anything different, parents not getting along or fighting. But thinking about it, realizing that I don't have many friends who had supportive relationships at home, I realized that it really was a big part of my family life.

My Dad, he's more of a chill person, but he cares, and he's always joking, he's fun, he's just not going to ask you about your life constantly. It's my Mom who asks about my life a lot, that's just the kind of person she is. It's a nice dynamic in the house.

> *It's always been our family tradition that every Sunday we eat out. It's the only day of the week that we eat out. So we'll go buy food and if we don't actually eat out we'll bring it to the house. And we'll just all sit and have an actual family dinner. Just because a lot of times during the week it's not feasible to get us all around one table with everyone's competing schedules. Usually Sunday went something like we wake up, we get ready, we go to church, we come back, it's like two o'clock in the afternoon, we're all starving, so we all say, "Okay, FOOD!" It's really nice.*
>
> *My family didn't really go out that much, though we'd still sometimes be like, "Let's see a movie!" Or just watch a movie at home. Or just like, hang out. We did a lot of that too.*

Tone

Turning to the second dimension of family interactions, *tone*, I look at two overarching variables, each of which contains several components. The first is "parent support," and the second is "responsive and directive parenting."

- **Parent support**: *Do young people feel supported by their parents?* This variable combines five individual measures into what statisticians call a "scale." Two of the variables measure supportive parenting:

    - How often do parents help their children to do things that are important to their children?
    - How often do they praise their kids for doing well?

  Contrastingly, three of the variables measure *unsupportive* parenting:

- How often do parents cancel plans with their children for no good reason?
- How often do they blame their kids for their own problems?
- How often do they criticize their children or their ideas?

These last three are "reverse coded"—that is, the higher the numbers, the lower the degree of supportive parenting. Kind of like golf, higher scores mean a worse round. So when I talk about supportive parenting I'm talking about the young people who *don't* report parents canceling plans, being blamed for problems, or being criticized—but who *do* report parents helping and praising them. And vice versa for unsupportive parenting.

Having parents who help children with things that matter to them, celebrate their successes and ideas, and follow through with plans can go a long way in supporting children towards achieving goals. When I talk about *parent support* in the coming pages, I'm talking about this whole bundle of variables—I'm analyzing the combined effect of these supportive parent behaviors.

In their own words:
Parent support for first-generation students
from an Asian female from the West

My Dad is a tailor. When I was little he had three jobs: he was working as a tailor in town, then he was working at another tailor far away, and he was working at a car dealership. He did all these jobs because he wanted to make sure that my Mom could always be there for us kids, always making our lunches, always going to all the parent-teacher conferences, all those things.

When I was a little bit older my Dad ended up buying his first store. That was really exciting, though he couldn't run the business from where we lived, he had to move to another state to keep the business going. He moved by himself because he wanted to make sure that my siblings and I stayed in the same area. My town had a pretty good schooling system, the public schools were pretty good, and my Mom didn't want to uproot us. My Dad would actually drive back and forth, he would just live in his store during the week and be with us on weekends. That was really hard. But he would always call us every night and ask us about school and everything.

Me and my siblings were all at different schools, and my Mom had to circle around to drop us all off and pick us all up every day, she wanted to make sure she got us all on time, that she wasn't late. My Mom would always make us lunch every day, and then she'd pick us up and she would always have snacks in the car, and then we would all do homework around the same table, then stop to do dinner together, and then if we were done with our homework we would go play together.

Or, because I used to be up late studying all the time—sometimes until one or two in the morning—my Mom would come up and bring me a snack and make me tea, and say, "Get some sleep, and then wake up and finish working." I'd always be like, "Thanks Mom."

Eventually my Dad got a store that was only forty-five minutes away from home so that was good. That was easier. My Dad's just trying to pay for us to all get through college. He told my sisters not to worry about their student loans, he's gong to work even harder to pay it off. It's crazy. Both my sisters work part-time, and I work part-time too so I can help with the bills. But it's still not enough.

My Dad is a man of very few words. He doesn't often say he's proud of you. He's just not that kind of guy. But the day he dropped me off for college I started crying because he said, "You make me so proud." And I was just crying because I was going to miss my parents, I'm the farthest away from home

> *of my siblings. I was like, "I don't know if I can do this!" But my Dad was like, "I am so proud of you. You can do this. Whatever you do here is going to be good." So I was like, "Okay, I can do this, that's motivation." My parents give me motivation.*

Now on to the second dimension of family tone:

- **Responsive and directive parenting**: *Do parents practice a combination of responsive yet directive parenting, fully engaging with children?*

This one seems especially important when we're talking about defining effective parental behavior. Responsive and directive parenting don't always go hand-in-hand. You've probably seen parents who are responsive but not directive: they'll help their kids do anything, but they don't provide any practical guidance for what will make a difference for their future. "You want to make an in-depth study of lint? Well, okay!" "You want to become a philosopher of philosophy? Sounds good!"

Alternatively, some parents give their kids lots of direction, but don't respond to their strengths and interests. Imagine: "You can get back to the books I want you to read when you've finished the dishes"; or, "If I'm going to pay for college, you're going to become a doctor. End of discussion." In addition, there are parents who just aren't that involved, neither responding to their children's interests nor providing direction.

Research shows that combining these two components of parenting—being both responsive *and* directive—works best. This relates to the "concerted cultivation" vs. "natural growth" discussion in the last chapter. Youth seem to benefit most from parents who both respond to their strengths and interests *and* help to guide them. "You're interested in music philosophy? That sounds really interesting, though it could be tough to find work in that field. Let's think about what careers might tap into that interest." Or "It sounds like you're more interested in computers than medicine. Tell me what you find interesting about them? I'm curious what you might be able to do with your college degree when you're done."

In the NLSY97, responsiveness is measured by whether young people report that parents are very supportive, somewhat supportive, or not very supportive, and direction is determined by whether they report that parents are strict about making sure they do what they are supposed to do. Again, these are approximations of the broader concepts I was trying to measure, but they nevertheless provide insight into an important component of family interaction.

In their own words:
Responsive and directive parenting
from a Hispanic female from the Midwest

Since I've been at college I've gotten a better sense of what I want to do. When my parents and I have longer conversations on the phone now, it is pertaining to that. My Mom will ask me, "Why don't you become a computer scientist? I hear they earn very well!" And I'll be like, "Mom, that's great, but that's not me." But it does lead to general conversations about the field, like the sense I have of what I want to end up doing.

And from another student,
an *Asian male from the West,*

My parents were comfortable with the fact that I was responsible and could stay out of trouble. Probably the one thing that they were a bit more invasive about was with drugs. My mom once asked a doctor to "sneak in a drug test" along with my regular blood tests. I had an idea what was going on, and I just told her straight up, "I don't do drugs, so I'll do the drug test voluntarily." She stopped bugging me about it afterwards.

And from another student,
an *Asian female from the West,*

> *My parents are super supportive. The only time my parents weren't really supportive of something was when my Dad didn't want me to enter the military. And my Mom wouldn't say it specifically but I knew she also didn't want me to do it. And I respect my parents, and I knew they had what's best for me in mind, so I was like, "Okay, I won't do it now. And if when I graduate I still want to do it I can do it then." And now that my siblings and I are in college they let us do what we want. One of my sisters doesn't always make the best life choices, and my Mom constantly worries about her, both of my parents do. And they've talked to her about it, but she just wants to do her own thing right now. And they're like, "You know what, that's okay, you can do what you want, but if you need help or if something goes bad, we'll be here for you."*

Substance

I've now provided a sense for the first two dimensions of family interactions, opportunity and tone. Let's turn to the third, *substance*. I analyze the substance of family interactions with three overarching variables: family conversations, parent involvement, and enriching environments.

- **Family conversations**: *How often do young people ask their parents for advice about school or job decisions, or discuss goals and aspirations?*

This is another "scale," meaning that it combines multiple survey questions into a single measure. It includes how often young people asked their parents for advice or help on education, training, or job decisions, and how much parents know about their child's goals and aspirations in life.

This variable taps into the kinds of conversations families have, including those in which kids ask their parents about academic and career decisions, and parents listen to them as they share their goals and aspirations. Through such conversations, students can gather more information about achieving their goals, or simply think through what their goals are and how they plan to achieve them. For parents with first-hand knowledge of college, these kinds of conversations could be a chance to pass on useful information. But even without such experience, these kinds of conversations offer a chance for parents and their kids to think through what they're striving for and how best to achieve it.

In their own words:
Family conversations for first-generation students
from a Hispanic female from the South

I think the main propellant I had through school was my parents. Especially my Dad, he put an emphasis on education, he always emphasized the importance of education. One of his biggest aspirations was just for us to go to school. For him it was always about taking advantage of opportunities.

My Dad always shared his dreams about going to school with us kids. My Dad really wanted to go school as a kid. He always told me, "Education is what's going to get you where you want to be. If you want to be somebody, education is probably the best route. Otherwise you're going to have to strike it lucky somewhere, and the likelihood of that is not that great."

But he also always said he would support us in our decisions regardless. For him it was always either: be in school, or work. Which meant he would support us as best he could through our educations. He said, "As long as I am able, I will support you in being where you need to be in terms of education." He said, "If you decide not to pursue an education, I will respect that, but keep in mind you'll have to work, I will not support you." So it was kind of the ultimatum: you go to school, or you're going to have to find a job. For the most

> *part he always pressed on us that he felt it was important and that he would be very happy if we pursued an education.*
>
> *Of course, my parents didn't really know about higher education. They didn't really know what "Advanced Placement" courses were, as far as they knew it was just advanced courses. When I was applying to college they didn't really understand that some colleges were better than others, to them a college was a college. It was kind of difficult explaining it to them.*
>
> *Once I started figuring out about different kinds of colleges, I would explain to my parents, "Some colleges have more resources, they're better than others." I've had three cousins go to college, two of them community colleges, and one of them a state college. And they all stayed in state. So no one had ever done what I've done, going to college out of state. But we're very close as a family, they're always first, they're still first. Moving so far away from family to go to college, at times it gets really hard. It can be really scary. But it's getting better.*

- **Parent involvement**: *How involved are parents—do they know their kids' friends, their friends' parents, their teachers, their whereabouts, and their school activities?*

This is the second component of substance, and based on another scale, tapping into a number of questions the sample of young people was asked about how involved their parents were in their academic and personal lives. These measured whether parents were connecting with their kids both socially and at school—such as knowing who their friends were, what their friends' families were like, how they were getting along with their teachers, what school and extra-curricular activities they were involved in, and what they were up to when not at school or home.

In their own words:
Parent involvement for first-generation students
from a Hispanic female from the South

My parents knew a pretty good portion of my friends, at least my close group of friends. All of us lived in the same district from my kindergarten year through high school. My Mom really got to know them.

When we were little, we had organized play dates and my Mom would see them. In middle school they would sometimes come over to my house. We would watch a movie or something and my Mom would meet them. In high school it was more along the lines of I would just tell my Mom I'm gonna be with them and she would remember them because I had been with them for so long. And when she would come for school activities or ceremonies she would meet them there too. She would remember them. My friends got to know my Mom really well because my Mom was the one who was at a lot of the events. And they all really loved her, my Mom's really goofy so they all loved her.

My parents always tried to make an effort at going to things that I invited them for. They didn't always have the opportunity to go—or they didn't always feel comfortable going.

But I remember my junior year when I became an honor student, we had a ceremony where they give you a sash and a certificate. And I remember telling my Mom to come. It was a very formal ceremony. We had to go on the stage and get our sash. And I remember seeing my Mom in the crowd and she was just smiling so hard. And afterwards I asked her, "Did you know what was going on?" And she said, "No, but just seeing you walk across the stage and get the sash, that was incredible!" I remember that.

I had an exorbitant amount of extra-curriculars. Probably more than it should have been! It was just so many club meetings. When I stayed a little late, sometimes they'd call me to be sure I was okay. They tried really hard to be as involved as they could.

- **Enriching environments**: *Does the family provide an enriching environment, such as the opportunity to take classes (e.g., music, dance, foreign language) or use a computer or dictionary at home?*

This is the third and final aspect of substance I examined. Expanding young people's horizons through classes, books, and computers is common in high socioeconomic status (SES) families, and creating this kind of enriching environment can make up for some of the knowledge less-educated parents lack.

In their own words:
Enriching environments
for first-generation students
from an Asian female from the West

When my siblings and I were younger my parents would read to us every single night. We would walk to the library all the time and pick out books. That's what we did for fun because we weren't really outdoors people, we weren't that into sports. And we couldn't really afford anything else. So we would just go to the library all the time and get books.

And another thing is that we all got into spelling bees. My sister, she was the oldest, so she started getting into it. And then we were all like, "Let's all get into it!" And my parents really liked it too because it's educational, a great way to learn more. So every time the spelling bee season came around they always gave us these big packets with the words we needed to learn. Every night my Mom would switch off quizzing us each separately with the spelling, and we all got really into that. One year we were even all in the same spelling bee. That was really fun. We were all really competitive. I think having all of my siblings really into education got me really into it too; it was like a fun thing. We were just raised to be like that. It was really great.

I know a lot of my friends would pay for SAT prep classes where they would have so much more help. And it was kind of intimidating sometimes because as a first-generation college student you can't afford all of these classes and you don't really know what it's about, but you just try to get through it.

My parents were really big on family time. Even more than just reading together and doing homework together, my parents just wanted us to have time together. My Dad would always take us to the lake or to the park or we'd go hiking together or things like that. Whenever we had the money he'd take us traveling, like one year we took a road trip to Philadelphia. He would take us to the zoo all the time. And now that we're older we appreciate it so much more because we've seen things in the world, and we've done things together. He always says, "Someday when you have families, I hope you take them to see things like that, because you bond."

Even when parents lack first-hand information about the education system, conversations about goals and aspirations can help keep their children focused; monitoring children's day-to-day interactions and activities can help keep them on track; and access to rich resources can help to bridge the knowledge gap between children from different socioeconomic backgrounds.

How do opportunities, tone, and substance relate to each other?

Now that I've walked you through the three dimensions of family relationships I looked at in my study—opportunity, tone, and substance—and how each is defined operationally, let's think through how they're related to each other in a little more detail. It's interesting to conceptualize how the different aspects of family relationships work together.

The primary benefit of opportunities for family interaction is to lay a foundation for whatever kinds of interactions a family is going to share. Without time together, tone and substance have no chance to emerge—there simply aren't interactions that can take on tone or substance. Put another way, opportunities for interaction lay the groundwork for *any* style of family interaction.

Tone then imbues the interactions that occur with feeling. It colors how a young person will receive them. There are positive and negative tones, which help to determine to what degree real communication can take place and the interaction can become substantive.

Indeed, both opportunities for family interaction and their tone can influence the substance of what is shared. Without time together, not a lot of substance is going to get through: parents can't be all that involved in their kids social and academic lives if they never spend time together, and conversations can't be all that rich if they're brief and infrequent. Likewise, an unsupportive or harsh tone can undermine an otherwise potentially substantive interaction. If parents know their kids' friends and teachers but are unnecessarily critical of them, or talk to their children about their education and goals but are unappreciative of their strengths and interests, and/or hostile toward their goals, this can weaken whatever substantive value might be gained.

In fact, I was able to examine exactly that: whether opportunities, tone, and substance build on each other, with opportunities paving the way for valuable tone and substance, and tone setting the stage for meaningful substance.

And I found that they do—to an extent. In statistical speak, the effect of opportunities is modestly "mediated" by tone, and the effect of both opportunities and tone is modestly "mediated" by substance. That said, measures of family relationships generally played a significant role independent of mediation as well: that is, opportunities, tone, and substance build on each other to some extent, and they also each individually support college-going, independent of each other.

What about factors beyond these measures?

Now let me step back for a moment and revisit a point that needs to remain fresh in mind. There are of course many factors in addition to family interactions that affect the likelihood of college going. I touched on some of these briefly in the first chapter. Now that I've explained just what I focused on in my study, let me elaborate on some other important factors that I have also considered in my analyses.

The first of these is *aptitude*. While this isn't the fixed entity it was once thought to be—environments in children's lives help to determine aptitude—it *is* to some degree based on genetic inheritance. The NLSY97 measured aptitude with a test called the Armed Services Vocational Aptitude Battery (ASVAB), which is a standard test of cognitive ability. As I stated before, in every analysis presented in this book, aptitude is "controlled," meaning that the relationships described hold across the spectrum from weak to strong student aptitudes.

Another factor that often comes up when I'm talking with people about this research is *immigrant families*. Such families may be particularly likely to share the kinds of supportive relationships I've discussed, and the children of immigrants may be particularly likely to become first-generation college students. Indeed, some of the research that inspired this project was research documenting the incredible lengths some immigrant families go to in supporting their children's upward mobility. However, because I wanted to study the role of family relationships across *all* American families—not just for immigrant families—I also controlled for immigrant status in every analysis presented in the book, including whether youth were born outside the United States ("first-generation immigrants"), or their parents were born outside the United States ("second-generation immigrants"). Here's a personal story in this vein…

In their own words:
An immigrant student's story
from a Hispanic female from the West

Since I was very little my parents—especially my Mom—she emphasized education a lot. When I was very little we lived in Mexico, and I remember she would make me go up on the roof to study, so I had a quiet place where I could learn. I think that's how it started off.

We moved to the States when I was eight. I didn't know any English when we moved but I was really eager and very excited to learn. Within a year I was in a regular English class. And so I slowly began to get the hang of school, and to do well. And I ended up doing really well. Like, in middle school I realized, "I can actually do this!" Perhaps my grades weren't the best earlier in school, but I was just like, "I'm doing my best and I want to learn!" That was my focus: I wanted to learn. I wanted to take advantage of the opportunities because we came to this country for opportunities.

Starting in middle school, whenever I could be part of the school play or student leadership or whatever, I was like, "I'm going to do this!" I kept telling my parents, "You brought me here for opportunity and I'm going to take advantage of this opportunity." They were very much supportive of me doing extracurriculars. I was able to do sports in middle school. In high school I dedicated a lot to my academics, but I also wanted to explore. I just wanted to be really involved, and I wanted to figure out what I actually liked. So I slowly began to get involved. I began to learn more about the opportunities within the high school.

Like, the second year of high school I wanted to run for a leadership position at school, not so much because I was going to win but because I just wanted the experience. My family helped me plan all this advertising and I had to come up with a slogan and everything. I got free candies from this warehouse and my family put all of these stickers on all of these candies we gave away for my campaign.

Another thing I remember is we got a computer when I was in sixth grade. It was a big deal for us. I don't think we got Internet until I was in high school. But my parents were very much like, "If you need something for school, you're going to buy it. I don't care how much it costs. If you need it and it's going to be helpful for you, then we're going to buy it." They knew how to use their money well. I never felt like I was missing something. They were just really smart shoppers. Looking back, I guess we never really traveled, we never really had vacations. But when it came to school supplies or things for projects it was a given, basically, that we would find a way to buy what I needed.

I emphasize the fact that I controlled for aptitude and immigrant status because they so often come up as questions. I also controlled for all the following:

- *Family income-to-poverty ratio.* This is one way statisticians look at family income, namely the ratio of total annual family income compared to the federal poverty level in any given year.

- *Parent education.* This was measured by children's residential mother's or father's highest year of education, whichever was higher.

- *Race/ethnicity*. Here, like the database I drew from, I used the following categories: non-Hispanic Black, Hispanic, Asian/American Indian/other, and non-Hispanic White.

- G*ender*. Female compared with male.

- *Cohort*. I analyzed two "cohorts," or age groups, in my NLSY97 sample, those who were age 13 or 14 at the start of the survey.

Why does it matter that I controlled for all these variables? The question here is whether family relationships meaningfully *predict* children's educational attainment, not whether they simply *co-vary* with them. For example, if supportive family relationships align closely with, say, family income, then it's possible that it's money, not family relationships, that explains young people's educational attainment. The same could be true for any of the above variables. This study addressed whether supportive family relationships help to explain children's educational attainment *apart from a family's income, parental education, youth's aptitude or immigrant status, or any of the other factors I statistically controlled for.*

Finally, it's worth taking a moment to mention that including parent education as an independent variable also allowed me to look at an additional question: whether supportive family relationships have a stronger effect for students with highly-educated or less-educated parents. Here's why that's interesting to look into:

On the one hand, educated families are likely to live in contexts that promote college in many ways. They tend to live in neighborhoods with better public schools and they are more likely to afford private schools. They also more often live in communities filled with adults who have attended college and communicate with children about their future higher educations and college-educated careers without a second thought (creating what sociologists call a "social norm" for college-going).

Educated families are also more likely to endow their children with cultural characteristics that communicate status—such as certain conversation styles, fashions, or interests which indicate though simple speech, self presentation, or casual conversation that someone *belongs* in educated circles, that they are bound for college. As earlier mentioned, Pierre Bourdieu first talked about the value of these symbolic characteristics as "cultural capital"—yet another form of capital passed down from one generation to the next.

In turn, first-generation students are less likely to have access to stellar K-12 schools, and they less often live in communities filled with college-educated adults. They are also less likely to be exposed to cultural characteristics like speaking styles, fashion, and extracurricular interests that seem to say, "I'm clearly bound for college." So while family relationships may be among many factors supporting kids in replicating their parents' college, family support may be more singularly responsible for first-generation students' success. Simply put: family relationships may matter more for first-generation students.

On the other hand, when educated parents build strong relationships with their kids, they are able to pass down their first-hand knowledge of how higher education works. While less-educated families can share relationships that promote success at school, they can't share their personal experience of how to apply for and succeed at college because they don't have that first-hand experience to draw on. For this reason, supportive family relationships could mean more for children raised in highly educated families. By analyzing what are called "interaction terms" between parent education and family relationships, I was able to look at the combined effect of different levels of parent education alongside different kinds of family relationships. I'll get to those findings in a bit.

There were lots of fascinating statistical analyses to explore in the NLSY97, and I've had fun with it. Though, as I've explained, I still can't claim causal connections because that kind of research isn't possible with this kind of study. But I've done everything possible to examine whether these findings are valid.

If you're interested in more information on the data and analyses used in this study, check out the appendix at the end of the book. This chapter has covered the precise questions these young people were asked in the NLSY97, which I will analyze in the coming pages. The chapter has also described the factors I controlled for to be sure the effects I saw for family relationships can't be explained by youth's aptitude, race/ethnicity, gender, immigrant status, or their parents' education or income.

Now let's turn to Chapter 6: What I learned about whether and how family relationships matter for young people who make the jump to become the first generation to go to college.

Chapter 6

Family Relationships Matter

The last chapter explained the variety of characteristics in family relationships that I examined, including the opportunities for interaction, their tone, and their substance. This chapter will focus on each of these dimensions as they relate to educational achievement. Take a look at Figure 9, which reports the proportion of young people with a given kind of family relationship. The first two bars cover opportunities, the next two bars tone, and the final three bars substance.

Figure 9 makes clear that valuable family relationships are more common among more educated youth. Progressing from students with no college (light gray bars), to some-college (charcoal bars), to four-year college (black bars), college-going youth increasingly report having both parents at home, fewer siblings, supportive parents, responsive *and* directive parents, family conversations about education and goals, parental involvement in their academic and social lives, and enriching environments.

Figure 9: Educational attainment disaggregated by family relationships

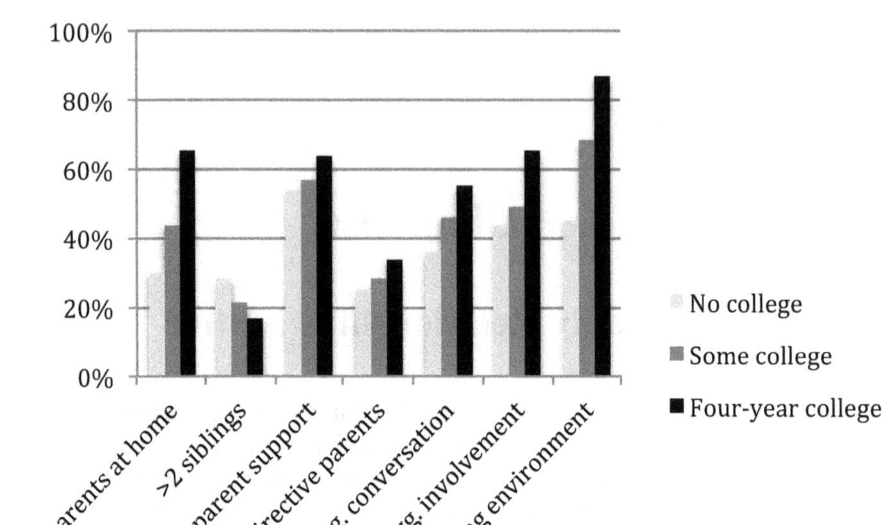

Note that three of these variables indicate either-or pairings: a) whether both parents were present; b) whether there were more than two children in the home; and c) whether parents practiced a combination of responsive *and* directive parenting (as opposed to one or the other, or neither). For the other family variables, percentages indicate the proportion of youth with more than average family interaction, such as those with above average parent support, family conversations, and so on.

I use the average as a marker because it is inherently meaningful, while the values assigned to these variables are not. That is, parent support and involvement do not naturally take on numerical values; they are only meaningful in a relative sense, such as whether youth who achieve high educational levels report experiencing more than the typical level of support.

While all these family relationships show clear correlations to college going, the degree of difference is particularly striking for some:

- First, more than twice as many four-year college students have both parents at home (65%) as do no-college students (30%). Here's one student's story…

In their own words:
Appreciating parents' presence
from a White female from the West

I spent a lot of time with my family growing up. They tried to have dinner together as a family. Both of my parents run their own businesses. Which was nice because my Mom worked out of the house so she was always around. I mean she was busy, but she was around. So even if she was busy there was always someone there when I got home from school. If I needed someone there was always someone there. And since my Dad ran his own business his time was always flexible. And the emphasis was always "go to college, go to college."

- Second, nearly twice as many four-year college students have above-average enriching environments (87%) as no-college students (45%). Again, an example…

In their own words:
Appreciating an enriching environment
from a White female from the West

I started playing piano when I was a little kid. When I was little my Mom would say, "Don't forget to practice!" But it became something I really loved so they didn't have to remind me. I think they saw I learned to love to do it. I took piano lessons all the way through high school. Looking back, there are so many sacrifices my parents made, and that was just one: paying for my piano lessons.

I had a hand-me-down piano from an aunt. When I got a little bit older they actually bought me a nicer piano for my birthday, at a discount store that was having a special. When they gave it to me, they had a family friend drive me home from school, and I remember being really annoyed because I was like, "It's my birthday! And I have homework to do! I have to get home!" And the family friend was like, "No, I just need to do a couple of things on the way." I guess my parents were getting it all set up for me. And when I finally got home my Mom was like, "Go in the front room..." and I went in and I was like "Oooh my gosh!!" I couldn't believe it. My parents still have the piano now. I play it when I go home. They saw that piano was something I really wanted to do, so they made the sacrifice.

Then, every summer I'd do a couple day camps, or one week at overnight camp. I was in Brownies, so when I was little there was a one-week day camp that was part of that. I think my Mom put me in Brownies because she'd been in Brownies and so she thought it was something that I would like to do. Another day camp she must have found out about through church or something. It was awesome. It was a really positive experience. So when I was younger I kept busy with stuff my Mom found out about for me.

We did have a computer. And we also had a typewriter. I remember typing on the typewriter for my assignments in middle school. I had to use that old-fashioned correction fluid to go back and correct things. We had that until I was twelve or thirteen. And then one of my best friends from grade school, her dad did something to do with computers, and he convinced my parents to buy a newer computer. So in high school I had a computer that had Microsoft Word, so I could type things.

Plus I was a voracious reader as a kid, I just loved it. And my Mom was like, "Great!" She kept buying me books at yard sales and thrift stores, she was always like, "Here's another book for you!"

We as a family went camping for a week every summer, and went boating. That was always a happy memory, spending time with them. My Mom, when we got older like in high school, we would spend time just one on one. We'd go to the movies together, or go to the beach. And junior and senior year of high school I started appreciating it more, because I wasn't so focused on spending time with friends. I was like "I'm going to leave home for college soon, I want to spend time with her."

• Somewhat less striking but nevertheless clear, about a fifth more four-year college students have lots of family conversations about education and goals (55%) and parent-involvement (65%) compared to no-college students (36% and 44%, respectively). Again, in one such student's words…

In their own words:
Appreciating parent involvement
from a Hispanic female from the South

I was president of one club. And at the end of the year we recognized the achievements of our students. I remember telling my parents to come, but my Mom didn't want to come by herself because she knew I would be busy running it. And I remember it being my Dad's birthday, and my Dad was getting out of work at the same time the event was starting so he couldn't have made it.

But just as the ceremony was starting to wind down, they made it anyways. Both of my parents came even though they were late, even though they had no idea what was going on, they came regardless.

My parents were just so...they looked so happy. It was just incredible to see them there. I was so touched. I mean, it was my Dad's birthday! But he'd just gotten off work, showered, and came!

Throughout my academic career it was my Dad who often couldn't come because he worked so much, but any chance, any ceremony he was invited to, he was always really excited to go. It's like it was not an option in their minds for them not to come.

Digging deeper into the data

The above data represent simple correlations, or *descriptive* relationships. Now I would like to move on to *predictive* relationships. While the two are often related, they aren't the same. Two factors can co-vary without one being meaningfully related to the other. For example, the San Francisco Giants indicates have won the World Series three times recently, all in even-numbered years. Does this mean they're likelier to win their next World Series in an even-numbered year? Of course not.

So now I move from descriptive to predictive relationships. I look at each of the three main components of family relationships individually: opportunity, tone, and substance. I won't go into details about the statistics here (if you're interested, I primarily performed multinomial logistic regression, and I've included details in the appendix). Regardless, one thing I should mention is that the book only presents statistically significant results, meaning the data in which there's less than a 10% chance that the relationship I'm showing doesn't actually exist in the population (and for most there's less than a 5% chance—or often a 1% chance). In other words, to simplify things I've filtered out data where connections didn't show up as statistically significant.

Another important point to revisit here is that four of the variables I analyze exist along a continuum—that is, they're not either-or variables (like having both parents at home, or not). Instead they're continuous variables, including supportive parenting, parent involvement, family conversations, and enriching environments. Since these variables exist along a gamut, I look at how a *standard deviation* increase in each relationship changes the odds of college going.

For example, if I say that increased parent support improves the odds of attending four-year college by 46%, what I mean is that each *standard-deviation increase* in parent support statistically significantly improves the odds of attending four-year college by 46%. But it would get pretty tedious to write out "standard deviation" and "statistically significant" every time I talk about a variable, so instead I'm telling you now: for continuous variables, I'm always talking about the effect of a standard-deviation change, and I'm only talking about statistically significant changes.

Keep in mind that I was looking at outcomes in my final year of data, when youth were 23 to 24 years old. By this time, the vast majority of students in the study who attended college had graduated. But since a few still hadn't (2% of the sample was comprised of college legacies still enrolled, and 4% was comprised of first-generational students still enrolled), to be conservative I continue to call these "four-year college students" or "bachelors students" rather than bachelor's degree earners, even though almost all have in fact earned a bachelor's degree by this point.

Finally, I'll be talking about five intergenerational educational trajectories in this chapter: "bachelor's legacies," who follow in their parents' footsteps to attend four-year college; "first-generation bachelor's," who become the first in their family to attend four-year college; "some-college legacies," who replicate their parents' some-college attainment; "first-generation some-college students," who become the first in their family to attend any college; and "no-college legacies," who replicate their parents' attainment of high school or less.

Now let's turn to the data (for me, the fun part): the effects of family relationships on first-generation college going. The next two figures illustrate the greater (or lower) odds of becoming the first-generation to attend some college (Figure 10) or four-year college (Figure 11) as compared to repeating parents' no-college education with each kind of family relationship. The baseline—at zero, where each of the bars begins—is where the odds of attending college or not are equal. Columns that rise above zero indicate increased odds of becoming a first-generation college student, while columns that fall below zero indicate lower odds of becoming a first-generation college student. The gridlines are presented at intervals of 0.2 to allow for comparison across figures.

Figure 10: The odds of being a *first-generation some-college student* with each family relationship (rather than a no-college legacy)

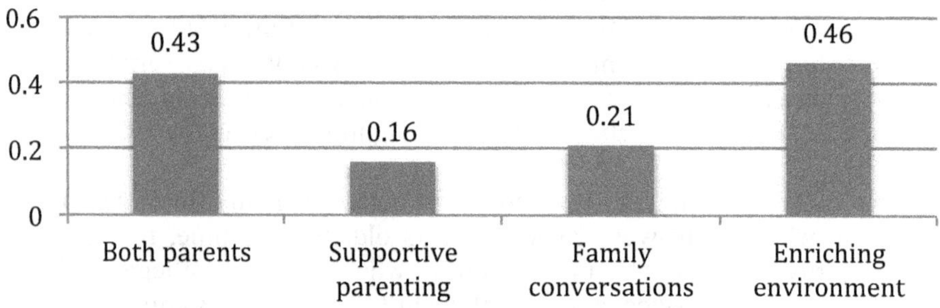

Note that just four of the variables are statistically significant for first-generation some-college students (Figure 10), and all in a positive direction. Figure 11 provides the same information for first-generation bachelors, and as you can see, even more family relationships have a significant positive effect there.

Figure 11: The odds of being a *first-generation bachelor* with each family relationship (rather than a no-college legacy)

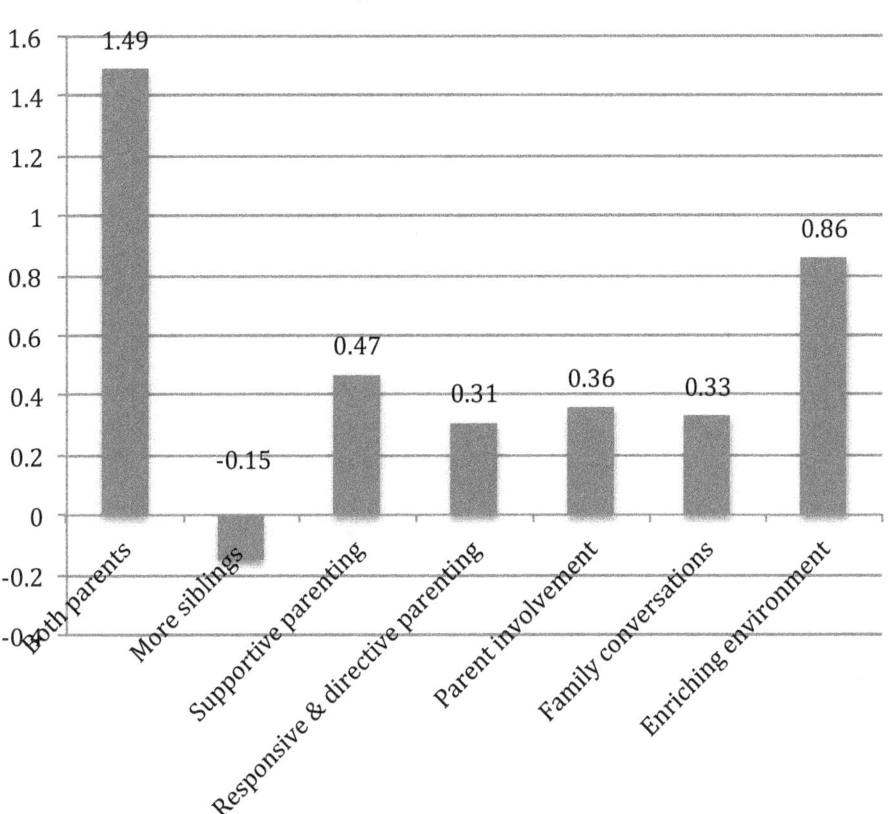

Opportunities for family interaction

Now let's take a look at each of the three main features of family relationships—opportunity, tone, and substance—and assess their influence on college going. Remember, the first two bars above—having both parents present and no more than two siblings—relate to opportunities. Family relationships rest on a foundation of shared time: if parents and children spend time together, they have the chance to develop strong bonds and to work together towards goals.

Having both parents at home fosters opportunities for family interaction by increasing the number of parent-hours available to each child. As Figures 10 and 11 clearly illustrate, this variable has a big effect, especially for attending a four-year college. Having fewer siblings in the home also has a modest effect on four-year college attendance, but substantially less than having both parents present. In the words of someone who experienced this…

In their own words:
Opportunities for first-generation family interaction
from a Hispanic female from the West

Growing up, my Mom always worked in the evening and my Dad worked in the morning. So for some time, whenever I would get home, it was just me, my Dad, and my sisters. I would eat with them, and then I would help him clean, and then take care of my sisters.

Then I think around sixth grade, when I started getting super involved at school, I think I would probably just get back from school and eat dinner. By then my Mom was working a day shift too. And even if my parents hadn't waited to eat with me, they would still be there with me while I ate, talking about my day. And then I would do my homework.

On the weekends we would always eat meals together, on Saturdays and Sundays for sure. My Mom always cooks. Especially on Sundays we'd have a routine where we went to church, and then we would go and get our groceries, go shopping as a family.

As I got busier in high school, sometimes I would need to stay home and do homework on Saturdays and Sundays, but then we would still all have dinner together later that day. We would always share our weekend dinners together.

The tone of family interactions

The second facet of family relationships is their *tone*: whether parents are supportive of their children, and whether they balance being both responsive *and* directive in their parenting. It has been hypothesized that a warm and engaged family environment helps children to focus on their education, while a harsh or apathetic one doesn't.

As Figures 10 and 11 show, a supportive relationship between parents and children means a lot: increased parent support improves the odds of becoming the first generation to attend some college by 16%, and four-year college by 47%. Likewise, Figure 11 shows that with responsive *and* directive parenting the odds of being the first-generation to attend four-year college improve by 31%. Thus the tone of family relationships significantly distinguishes first-generation college students from no-college legacies, with a particularly notable effect on four-year college attendance. Again, an example in a young person's own words…

In their own words:
Parent support for first-generation students
from a Hispanic female from the West

My parents, they were definitely very supportive. I mean, they didn't really know anything about the subjects I was studying, they really didn't. But they were very supportive of everything that I did. A lot of parents will tell you, "You need to do chores." But my parents were like, "If you need to do homework, do your homework." Or if they saw that I was really busy with extracurriculars, that was fine. I think for them it was like: school is first, and taking classes and doing my homework was the most important. So they were very supportive in that sense. And picking me up from rehearsal, and from practice, and from all these conferences as well. Just hoping I would get there safely, and hoping for the best for me.

The substance of family interactions

Lastly, let's look at the *substance* of family interactions, including whether parents are involved in children's social and academic lives, talk to their children about their aspirations, and provide an enriching environment (presented in Figures 10 and 11).

Parent involvement is only significant for first-generation bachelor's students, for whom it improves the odds of becoming the first generation at four-year college by 36%.[1] However, having more family conversations about youth's aspirations improves the likelihood of both being the first generation to attend some college by 21%, and four-year college by 33%. Strikingly, more enriching environments improve the odds of attending some college by 46%, and of being a four-year college student by a remarkable 86%! Here's an example…

> ***In their own words:***
> ***Enriching environments for the first-generation***
> *from a Native American female from the West*
>
> *My parents would always get me the sports equipment I needed when I really had to have it. Like I remember one year the toe sort of ripped open on my shoe. And my Mom was very supportive, she got me new shoes the very next day. It was something that I really needed and I really appreciated it. I knew that expensive shoes were a big burden on her. I never took for granted the fact that she would do something like that. It meant a*

[1] Let me elaborate on this finding with a rather important statistical detail: Most family relationships in the NLSY97 were measured in both early- and late-adolescence, and they have similar effects at these two times. Throughout the book I have presented effects of family relationships in late-adolescence. However, parent involvement only has a statistically significant effect for first-generation bachelors as measured in *early-adolescence*, at which time it improves the odds of attending college by over a third. Therefore, for this one bar in this one figure, I present findings from a regression analyzing the effects of early-adolescent family relationships on first-generation college going.

lot.

We had a lot of books at home. We have a lot of bookshelves. My Dad, he would really like taking us to bookstores and us picking out books to read.

And we do have one computer. My Mom got it for us. It kind of was a big deal. It's shared among the whole family, which would make doing work really hard, because I would have to share it among my older sister, myself, and my younger sister. We were all of age in school where you really need a computer for homework. We'd call dibs, really. I have like a thousand dollar laptop now at college, which I cherish so much because I really need it. But I think it was a really big burden for my Mom to buy it.

What about youth who *replicate* parents' college attainment?

In Figures 10 and 11 I looked at the effects of family relationships on becoming the first generation to attend college. But what about youth who replicate their parents' college going—do these same family relationships matter in families with a history of attending college?

The answer here is simple: Yes, absolutely. I found that family relationships matter for young people's educational attainment regardless of whether they are the first in their families to attend college or are following in their parents' footsteps. Previous research has suggested the great value of strong family relationships for college legacies, and my work clearly aligns with this finding. The exact effects of family relationships on replicating parents' college are presented in the next two figures, Figures 12 and 13.

Figure 12: The odds of being a *some-college legacy* with each family relationship (rather than a no-college legacy)

0.6
0.4
0.2
0
0.21
0.49
0.27
0.5
Supportive parenting
Responsive & directive parenting
Family conversations
Enriching environment

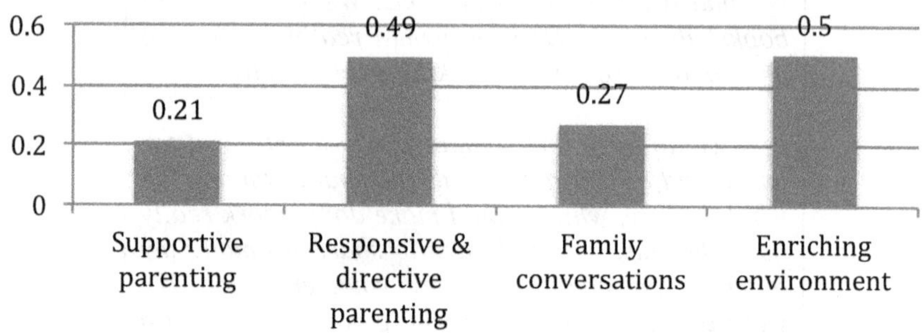

Figure 13: The odds of being a *bachelor's legacy* with each family relationship (rather than a no-college legacy)

1.6
1.4
1.2
1
0.8
0.6
0.4
0.2
0
-0.2
-0.4
1.44
-0.31
0.6
0.9
0.27
0.42
0.77
Both parents
More siblings
Supportive parenting
Responsive & directive parenting
Parent involvement
Family conversations
Enriching environment

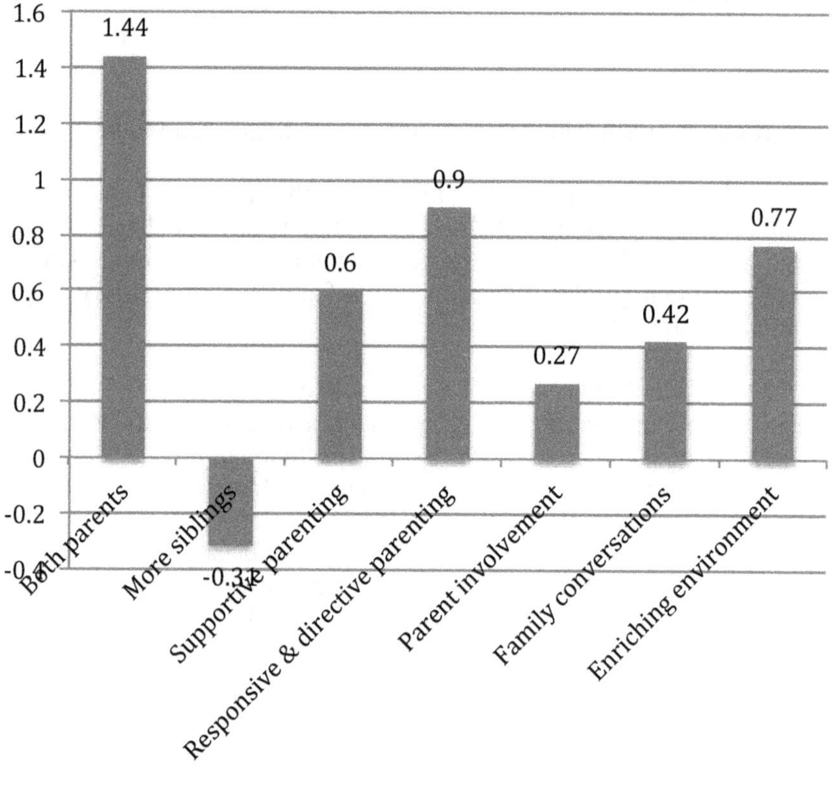

As you can see from comparing Figures 12 and 13, the size and significance of effects are not identical to those for first-generation students. In fact, as I outlined in the last chapter, in some additional analyses I looked at the effect of family relationships combined with more and less parent education (statistically speaking, I analyzed interaction variables between parent education and family relationships).

Here's what I found: while valuable family relationships strongly predict first-generation college going, they do so even more strongly in families with a history of going to college.

This combined effect makes sense, given that as college educated parents interact with their children, not only may they help to focus their children on academic achievement, they may also pass on their first-hand knowledge of how higher education works. Less educated families lack that first-hand understanding of how to apply for, succeed at, and graduate from college. So even when they encourage their kids' interests and help keep them focused on their goals, they simply don't have that first-hand knowledge to pass down.

Thus there *are* differences in how family relationships matter for first-generation versus college-legacy students. If strong family relationships are meaningful for first-generation students, they are even more so for those with college-educated parents. But the take home message is the same: valuable family relationships powerfully predict young people making it to college.

In summary

The opportunities, tone, and substance of family interaction each play an important role in predicting intergenerational educational attainment. Measures of family relationships predict reaching both some college and four-year college, though they have broader effects for four-year college going. That's a powerful set of findings. Again, underscoring these findings, here's someone talking about their personal experience in this respect…

In their own words:
Parents support children's attainment
from a Hispanic female from the Midwest

My parents always told me, "You call us when you're done at school, or with your activities, and we'll pick you up." Even if they were in the middle of a meal or out doing errands, they would just stop and pick me up. And that was really nice because I had a lot of friends who, even in the middle of a snowy winter, they would have to walk home by themselves. But my parents never complained about helping me. They never said, "We have to go pick her up again?! Maybe she should just take the bus!" It was never like that. It was always like, "Okay, we'll come pick you up no matter where you are, no matter what we're doing." As long as I was doing school activities, they always said, "We'll pick you up." That was nice.

I also remember they came to see me at a competition my senior year of high school, and my Dad took out his phone and started taping me. And then when we visited his family this summer he would randomly pull out his phone and show his family the video. He'd be like, "Look! Look! Look what she's doing! That's my daughter!" I could tell he was proud of me. A lot of times my parents don't vocalize how proud they are, but I can tell by their actions. I've heard them talking on the phone, they'd be in the living room and I'd be in my room but I'd hear them saying, "I went to see my daughter do this!" or "She got into this college!" It was subtle but it was always there. I was always supported. Which I think was really important. It was really nice.

Chapter 7

Falling Short of College

In the previous chapters I've shown how supportive family relationships can promote first-generation college attendance, just as they perpetuate educational success from one generation to the next. But as you'll recall, almost as many young people fell short of their parents' college educations as exceeded them. Can strong family relationships reduce downward mobility?

Let's revisit the numbers first. A total of 24% of students fail to replicate their parents' four-year college education (15%) or some-college attendance (9%). Despite the fact these youth's parents have first-hand knowledge of the higher education system, and most of their families have higher than average incomes (recall Figure 6), these young people are slipping through the cracks of higher education.

Those are the raw facts, and facts are stubborn things. Don't they suggest there is nearly as much reason for pessimism as optimism? Isn't this trend as discouraging as the upwardly mobile trend of the last chapter is encouraging? Are we really making progress?

There is an alternative view. This book explores the impact a family can have on the educational trajectory of its children. I've shown that for the majority of young people who either replicate their parents' education or exceed it, family relationships are an important factor. For young people on the down escalator rather than the up one, could family relationships play a role too? Might strong family relationships protect against downward educational mobility, just as they promote upward educational mobility?

To keep the definitions of each of these intergenerational educational trajectories fresh in mind, recall that I use the term "legacy" to refer to youth who follow in their parents' footsteps to attend four-year college ("bachelor's legacies"), some college ("some-college legacies"), or no college ("no-college legacies"). I refer to youth who become the first in their family to attend college as "first-generation"—either reaching four-year college ("first-generation bachelor's") or some-college shy of four-years ("first-generation some-college students"). Lastly, I refer to youth who fall short of their parents' college attainment as "downwardly mobile"—either failing to replicate their parents' four-year college attainment ("downwardly mobile bachelor's") or some-college attainment ("downwardly-mobile some-college students").

Take a look at Figure 14. It shows that downwardly mobile students (illustrated by the two checkered bars) are less likely than college-bound students to share supportive family relationships. Notice that the bars tend to peak on the left and slope down towards the right for each valuable family characteristic (with one exception—having more than two siblings—where, predictably, the reverse slope is observed). While college legacy and first-generation college students commonly report lots of valuable family interactions, downwardly mobile and no-college legacy students are less likely to do so.

In short, valuable family relationships are associated with a lower likelihood of downward mobility. In this chapter I'll make an even stronger case for this idea. For parents who face this situation—offspring who for whatever reasons are leaning away from going to college—the information in this book is just as empowering as for those who want to help their child become the first to attend college. If you're a parent getting the feeling that your child is straying from the college path, and you want to encourage college going, this book is also for you.

Figure 14: Family relationships for youth who follow each intergenerational educational path

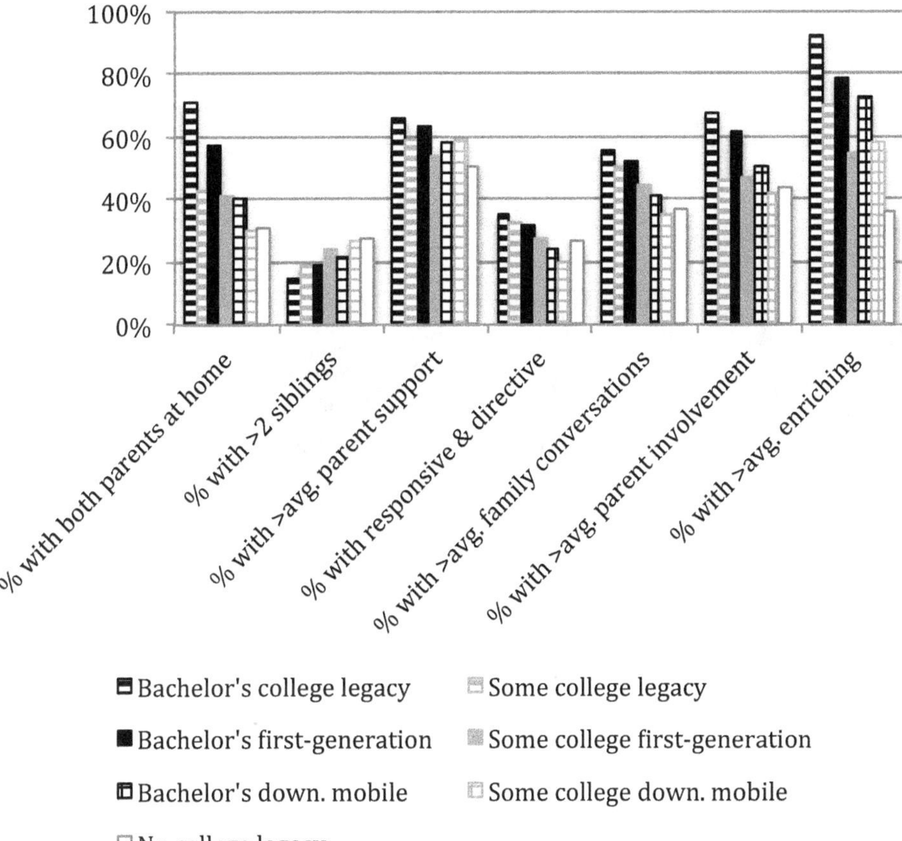

Let's examine the numbers more closely, keeping in mind the three aspects of family interactions: opportunities, tone, and substance. As you'll recall, *opportunities* includes whether both parents are present and how many children live in the household. *Tone* includes parent support and a combination of responsive *and* directive parenting. And *substance* covers parent involvement in their kids' academic and social lives, family conversations about education and goals, and enriching learning environments.

Take a look at the next two figures. Figure 15 illustrates students who don't attend college at all though their parents did, and Figure 16 looks at those who fall short of four-year college even though their parents achieved this level of education. For each family relationship, columns that rise above zero indicate *lower* odds of downward mobility, while any columns that fall below zero indicate *greater* odds of downward mobility.

Figure 15: Reduced odds of falling short of some-college

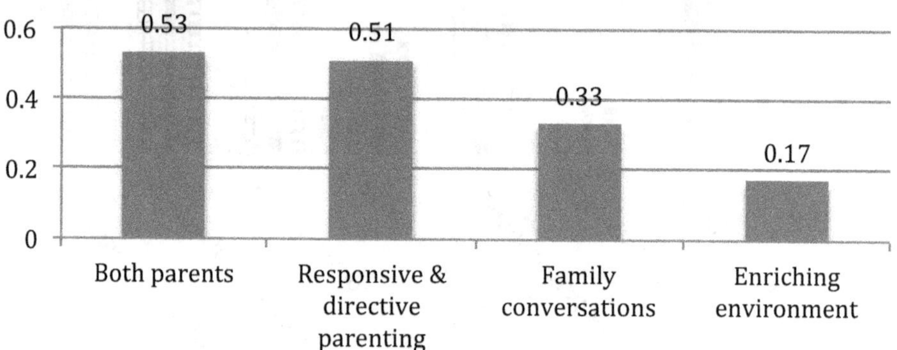

Figure 16: Reduced odds of falling short of four-year college

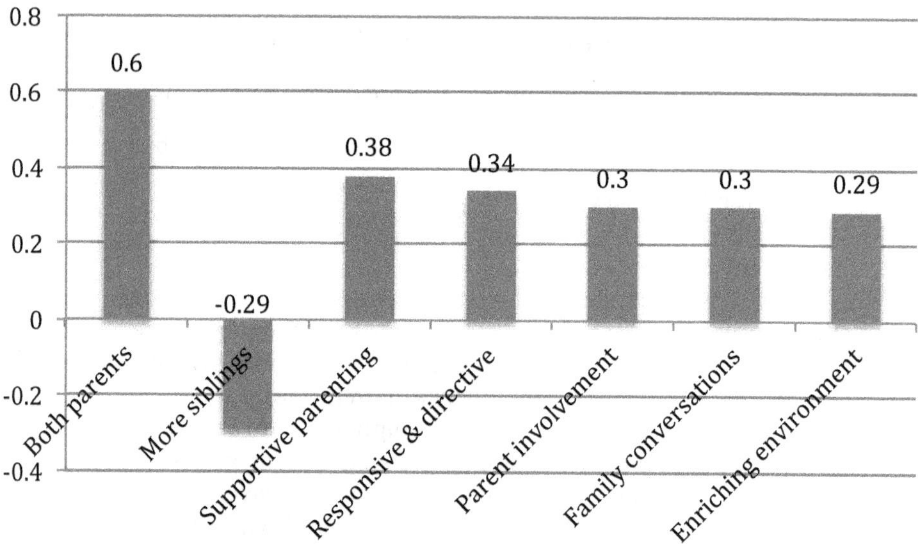

What do these two figures show? Looking at opportunities for family interaction first, having both parents present makes a big difference, reducing the odds of falling short of some-college by 53%, and of falling short of a bachelor's education by 60%. This means that if both parents are present the chances of a child being downwardly mobile are reduced by more than half. The number of siblings also matters for bachelors' mobility: the odds of falling short of a bachelor's education are reduced by 29% with fewer siblings. To combine these, two-parent families with fewer children have a *big* advantage.

What about family tone? Unlike parent and child numbers in the family, which are likely to be a given by the time you have offspring in high school, these behaviors are more within a parent's control. Looking first at the degree of parental support, this clearly matters for bachelor's attainment: when parents support their children's interests, the likelihood of them failing to replicate their parents' bachelor's education is reduced by 38%. Likewise, the research discussed in Chapter 4 showed that when parents were both responsive *and* directive it was good for their kids' outcomes. This refers to responding to your children's interests and perspectives *and* being firm in steering them in positive directions. A combination of responsive and directive parenting appears to have a big impact on college attendance: it reduces the odds of falling short of some-college by over half (51%), and it reduces the odds of falling short of a bachelor's education by over a third (34%).

> ***In their own words:***
> ***Parents protect kids' achievements***
> *from a Hispanic female from the Midwest*
>
> *My Mom has always wanted us to be a really tight knit family. She was really connected to us all. She would pick me up from school every single day. My school was like three blocks from my house, but every single day she would pick me up either walking or in the car. She didn't really leave me room for misadventures, which in retrospect I think was a good thing.*

My older brother, I guess he was kind of a troublesome child. He was a troublemaker; he was actually malicious in a lot of ways. And so my Mom, she put him in soccer, she put him in all these things so he wouldn't have time for anything else. Because she saw glimmers in him that could go completely the wrong way. And I think that reinforced her need to constantly be checking on all of us, to be like "What are you doing, who are you with?" Even now that I'm at college she calls me almost every night just to be like, "Hey, what are you doing, how are you doing?" It's like a five-minute conversation, but she still calls me every day.

Ever since I was young, my Mom always made education a big part of what she emphasized for us. We had a family friend who always said that her kids would all go to college, get an education. And when my Mom heard that, she remembers thinking, "Well if her kids are going to do it, my kids are going to do it too!" So when I was growing up my Mom was always like, "Oh, great, you got an A! But why isn't that an A+?" So there was always that expectation. It was nice having that.

And my Mom was never the type of person where she'd be like, "Oh you're with that person, do whatever you want!" Because I know some friends' parents would just love a certain person and would let their kids do whatever when they were with that person. But my Mom was never like that. My Mom would always try to have friends come over to my house rather than having me go to their house. I would be like, "Mom, can I go to so-and-so person's house?" And she'd be like, "Just tell them to come here! Tell them to come here!" So we spent a lot of time at my house.

Once my Mom got more comfortable with my friends and saw that they were good people I think that's when a lot more freedom did come for me. I never got into any major trouble. My friends were similar in perspective to me. So I think it got easier for her to think, "You know what, it's okay, she can go out a little more."

What about the substance of family interactions: parents' involvement in children's academic and social lives, family conversations about education and goals, and an enriched environment? To recap these variables, *parent involvement* entails such things as whether parents know their children's friends, their friends' parents, their teachers, and what they're up to in school. *Family conversations* relates to whether they talk to their offspring about education and goals. And *enriched environments* are those in which students can take classes such as art or music and where the home has resources such as dictionaries and computers.

Looking at the data on these variables in Figures 15 and 16, having involved parents reduces the odds of failing to replicate parents' four-year college education by 30%. In turn, parent conversations with children about their education and goals helps prevent downward mobility for both some-college and four-year college (by 33% and 30% respectively), as does having an enriched environment in the home, which reduces the odds of some-college and four-year college downward mobility (by 17% and 29% respectively). In short, all of these behaviors play an important role in maintaining parents' educational achievement, and are within the ability of most parents to address.

In their own words:
Parents protect kids' achievements
from an Asian female from the West

When we got to high school, at first my parents were really strict about whether we could go to dances and things like that. But then they lightened up after a while when they realized that my sisters were really good, they weren't going to do bad things, they could trust them. And when I got to high school—I'm the youngest—they kind of let me do what I want, they gave me free reign. And I liked that because I knew I wasn't going to do bad stuff. I came home before 10 o'clock, I always got my homework done.

My home was always a hangout place for my friends and my brother's friends and all my sisters' friends too. When I was a freshman in high school my sister was a senior and we did this one program together. We'd have practices at my house, and my Mom would give us all snacks and everything. And then junior/senior year I got close to a group of girls and we'd always hang out at my house, and have sleepovers and stuff like that.

My parents liked it when we'd hang out at home so they could make sure we were safe. Even though my Mom trusted me she always worried that if I went somewhere else something would happen.

I remember my Mom wanted to set up our schedules, she wanted to make sure we had the same teachers, the same classes, that way we had better relationships with the teachers. She'd do things like that.

And my Mom got to know some of my friends' parents, and my parents would always tell me if they didn't feel comfortable with somebody. They would just tell me, "Be careful, I don't want you to become like that." If they did say something about someone I would take that advice.

My Mom has really good intuition I think. I usually listened to her, but there was this one time I didn't listen to her and she was just completely right. About a boy. She really knew. She would still let him come over and we'd do homework together and she'd let me go to the movies with him. But then she'd say, "You know, I'm not sure about him." I'd say, "It's okay Mom, it'll be fine," but afterwards he turned out to not be a very nice person. But my Mom never said, "I told you so." She just said, "It's okay, there'll be other boys."

To summarize, opportunities for family interaction, and the tone and substance of those interactions, *all* significantly protect against downward educational mobility. Having both parents in the home is an especially valuable guard for both some-college and bachelor's educations, and smaller family size contributes to the latter. Responsive *and* directive parenting is valuable in regard to family tone, as is supportive parenting for bachelor's achievements. And with regard to substance, being interested in children's academic and personal lives, talking with them about this and their educational goals, and providing an enriched environment all contribute substantially. Every one of these has a protective impact for young people with college-educated parents.

So, what's the bottom line? Family relationships relate not only to upward educational mobility but also to downward educational mobility. When more-educated families fail to share supportive relationships, their children are likelier to struggle in school and are less likely to attend college. This is true for parents with some college experience, and it is even more true for those with bachelor's educations. The predictive power of these variables is striking. These are the simple statistical findings.

In their own words:
Parents can shield against hard times
from a Hispanic female from the South

Middle school was a really tough time for me. Phew. I got really rebellious in my middle school years. It got to the point where I was even considering dropping out. I let my grades slip. In middle school it was really effortless to get A's, so to not get A's meant you really, really weren't doing anything. And I was getting C's.

My parents finally started to really worry about

me. At one point I was even telling my Dad, "I think I'm going to drop out when I can." By law I had to be 16 to drop out, so that wasn't going to be until my sophomore year of high school, and I wanted to drop out in middle school. But I thought, "Maybe I can make it until then."

And my Dad...he really pushed back. He said, "No, you can't drop out! Education is what's going to get you far! Do you need help? We'll get you help—we'll find somebody who can help!"

So I started re-prioritizing. I got my motivation again, just realizing again how much my parents went through to give me the life I have. Around eighth grade is when I started to get it together again. Freshman year of high school was still rough, I was still trying to figure it out. Middle school had never really involved homework so I wasn't really used to studying. It was kind of a swift kick that got me into studying. I was like, "Well, maybe I do need to study!"

Though throughout high school sometimes I would push myself too hard. I would get to the other extreme. I went from not trying enough, to trying too hard. I remember having a lot of breakdowns at the beginning of high school. A lot of nights where I'd just cry. It was just overwhelming.

I remember both of my parents coming to me, it would just depend who heard me. I'd think I was being discreet about it, but they would hear me crying. So my Dad would come in and hug me and try to console me, try to make me feel better. It was really nice to know that they were there for me.

I remember I felt like I was putting my parents through this stress, but I didn't mean to, I was just feeling really overwhelmed and sometimes isolated. As hard as I tried to explain it to my parents they didn't quite understand what I was going through, the anxiety. They always asked, "Why do you put yourself through this stress?" It was just a really difficult time.

I remember there were a lot of late nights when at two in the morning, three in the morning I would still be working. Almost every single night my parents would knock on my door and ask, "Are you okay? Can you go to sleep?" And I would say, "I just have to finish this and I'll go to bed." And they'd say, "Okay, but seriously go to bed as soon as you can!" Some days I would think, "They don't want me to do well!" But then other days I would realize, "No, they just really want me to be healthy."

Chapter 8

Conclusions and Implications

> ***In their own words:***
> ***Your legacy is your education***
> *from a Hispanic female from the Midwest*
>
> *A big thing that my parents always tell us is: "When we pass away, we're not going to leave you with much inheritance. We'll leave you what we have, but that's not your legacy. You're legacy is your education."*

The previous chapters give a picture of who goes to college, how much upward and downward mobility there is, whether college is worth the investment, and just how much family relationships can mean for college attainment. I've presented mountains of statistics as plainly as possible, and I've tried to bring these statistics to life with real stories from first-generation students who credit their accomplishments to their strong and supportive families. Let me offer a brief recap here, along with a discussion of some of the implications. I'll also interweave more of the words of the young people I interviewed into this review to help bring these findings to life one last time.

To begin, I based my empirical models on James Coleman's

theoretical work, and it's worth returning to his reasoning for a moment. Coleman argued that families shape children's educational development in three fundamental ways: by providing access to the skills and knowledge gained through higher education (*human capital*, typically measured via parent education); by providing access to better resources both within and outside the home (*financial capital*, generally measured by family income); and by providing family supports through relationships and interactions that help focus children on academic success. This third resource he characterized as *social capital*.

We know from decades of research that human and financial capital mean a lot for young people's outcomes. Countless studies have shown socioeconomic status (SES), as measured by parent education and income, to be one of the strongest and most consistent predictors of children's educational attainment. A large literature leads us to expect that children from less-educated, lower-income families will face serious barriers to attending college, while those from highly-educated and well off families are more likely to succeed.

But the concept of "social capital" both complements and complicates this picture. It's not enough simply to know a family's socioeconomic level. Coming from a high or low socioeconomic background can mean something very different for educational attainment, depending on the kinds of relationships shared in the family. This finding supports Coleman's decades-old argument that human, financial, and social capital stand side-by-side in influencing children's attainment.

CONCLUSIONS

Let's return to the simple statistic I presented at the start of this book: *half* of American youth are following a different educational path than their parents. Twenty-six percent of young people become the first generation in their family to attend college, while twenty-four percent fall short of their parents' college attainment. The kinds of family relationships that are shared powerfully predict educational movement in either direction, even when controlling for parent education, family income, children's aptitude, immigrant status, and more.

In a nutshell:

- Higher-achieving youth are more likely to experience valuable family relationships in adolescence.
- Multiple aspects of family interactions have a significant effect on whether young people attend some college or four-year college, including each of the following.
- *Opportunities* for family interaction are important. I examined opportunities for interaction with variables for having both parents at home and having fewer siblings, each of which can influence the number of parent-hours available per child.
- The *tone* of family interactions also matters, such as whether parents are supportive of their children, and whether they practice a combination of responsive and directive parenting.
- Finally, the *substance* of family interactions—as measured by the frequency of family conversations about education and goals, parent involvement in their children's academic and social lives, and the provision of an enriching environment—also has a significant effect.

These are consequential findings. While it wouldn't be good science to ignore family education and income in any modern study of youth outcomes, given their ubiquitous and overlapping influences, the findings in this book, based on a nationally representative sample of young people, clearly demonstrate a substantial, significant, and overlapping role for family relationships.

While parent education and family income tend to be established early in a child's life, often before they are born, family relationships are not. They begin essentially at birth, and are malleable over time. This fact provides an opportunity for *all* families, regardless of SES, to support their children's educations, and thereby their children's futures. Let me say it one more time, in the clearest possible terms: *across the spectrum of parent education and family income, sharing rich family relationships predicts educational success*.

> ***In their own words:***
> ***Family relationships interact with SES***
> *from a White female from the West*
>
> *My parents always joked, "We stopped being able to help you with school in the third grade." Which isn't true. But you know, by high school I was definitely doing stuff that they didn't remember or just had never learned. So at that age I wasn't asking them for help, but my Mom especially was always asking about what I was doing and I remember I'd have her proofread whatever I wrote because she was really good at finding typos. So they tried to stay involved that way. And my Mom always asked, "What are you working on, what are you doing?" And I would tell her about stuff I thought she would find interesting.*
>
> *My parents always knew about my schoolwork, especially if there was some kind of special project we had to work on at home. There were lots of group projects in middle school. My parents would always be really interested in helping out if it was some kind of hands-on thing. I remember in seventh grade there was some kind of special project, and my Mom stayed up with me the night before making the poster board with me. She helped me hand cut out all the letters and post them on the poster board for the display. And we got to school the next day and a lot of the other kids had just printed them out on the computer. At the time we didn't have a color printer. We just had one of the old-school dot-matrix printers. We didn't have a laser printer. And I remember my Mom feeling bad, being like, "These other kids could just print it, you had to cut yours out." Whereas I felt like, "You spent all that time with me, that made it special!"*

Of course, these findings don't deny the advantage of a high SES background. Recall that in Chapter 6 I described analyses showing that while valuable family relationships strongly predict first-generation college going, they have an even stronger effect in families with a history of going to college. This, too, was a common theme in my interviews with first-generation college students…

In their own words:
Socioeconomic status still matters
from a White female from the West

I knew it was important for me to go to college. But no one spent a lot of time talking about what actually happens at college. I didn't know you picked your own classes and had your own schedule and some things were going to be early in the morning and some things were going to be at night and you'd have all this time off in between. I remember getting to college and being like, "Oh, we're not on a high school schedule, we're not in set classes from eight to three."

And I was surprised at the range of things people had been exposed to before they got to college. And the way people would just casually drop names of writers or philosophers or whatever the thing was that they were interested in. I remember feeling intimidated by that, just like, "Wow, you really sound like you know what you're talking about. I don't even know what that thing is!" In high school I'd had a couple of friends who were interested in the same nerdy things as me, but in high school I'd never felt intimidated by people who I thought were that much smarter or had that much more access.

And there was also the issue of just feeling out of place in that environment. Even the way other students talked to professors—I just felt so

> *intimidated by that, especially at first.*
>
> *The whole thing with my family was "go to college, go to college." There wasn't a lot of conversation about what you do when you get there, and how you figure out what you want to study and what you want to do, and how do you spend your time during the summers. That kind of thing.*
>
> *All the stuff that gets passed down informally, I didn't get most of that. I mean, my parents just didn't know, they hadn't been, right?*

So it's not that social capital eliminates the effects of socioeconomic status; researchers have known family education and income were important for a long time. But it turns out these are inextricably intertwined with social capital. This is true in both positive and negative directions. High parent education can be magnified by sharing valuable family relationships. Or the advantages of high parent education can be lost if parents fail to provide needed family interactions. And most encouragingly, the challenges of low parent education can be overcome by sharing valuable family relationships.

How much do family relationships matter?

This book has presented an abundance of statistics and figures about how much family relationships can change the odds of going to college. Let's listen to the words of young people as they relate to several of the findings, summarizing what has been learned in the preceding pages.

- With both parents at home, or exposure to more enriching environments, the odds of children becoming the first generation to attend some-college increase by over 40%, and the odds of them having a four-year college education increase by over 80%.

In their own words:
Parents promote an enriching environment
from a Hispanic female from the South

My freshman year I was having a really hard time in algebra. I was extremely behind. I was not doing well. Some nights I was just breaking down, feeling really sad.

But the school had sent home packages about free tutoring for students who get free or reduced lunch, so my Mom was like, "What's this tutoring?" So I looked at it, and I was like "Wow, I could get tutoring for algebra!" So I started going to get tutoring twice or three times a week for algebra for free! My Mom made a big effort of taking me to that tutoring.

I was also taking chemistry, and I was behind in that too. But the free tutoring only covered one class. So my Dad said, "I will pay for the tutoring in chemistry." And I said, "But tutoring is really expensive Dad!" And he said, "It doesn't matter." I don't know how he did it, but he paid for a semester of tutoring in chemistry for me. And thanks to the extra tutoring I managed to do really well in that class. And in algebra. I mean, when I started the tutoring even passing was going to be really hard, but with all the tutoring I managed to pass the final. That was one of the instances where my Dad really came through. He told me, "I will find the money. I will work extra hours. You are going to get extra tutoring and you are going to pass these classes." I think that's one of the things I remember the most from high school.

I also remember when my class required me to buy a fancy calculator, one of those graphing calculators. My Dad was just like, "Why do they have to cost $100?" And I just told him, "I don't know Dad. But it's okay, I can borrow someone *else's. It'll be okay." But he said, "No" to that. My Mom and I managed to do some research, and we found one at a pawnshop, and they had barely marked it down, but my Dad insisted that I should have my own calculator. He insisted that I shouldn't have to borrow other people's things to do well in school.*

In terms of resources at home, we had a computer, and that computer was only bought because my cousin told my parents it was a necessity in school. Nowadays you can't do homework without a computer. And with my parents, anything that had to do with education, my Dad would go for it. If I said, "I need this," and he said, "For what?" if I said, "For school," he'd say, "Okay." So yeah, I had a computer. I didn't get a laptop until my senior year of high school, and that was because I had worked over the summer and bought it for myself. My Dad didn't see the necessity of a laptop. He'd say, "For what? You have a desktop." So I bought the laptop with my own savings.

And then thinking about the computer, I remember one night my computer wasn't working and I had to type up a paper for school. So I called my friend and I stayed over at her house really late to borrow hers. And my Mom, the entire time, waited in the car. I left at like two or three in the morning, and my Mom was out there waiting that whole time. Those are the moments that really stick out to me.

- With either more supportive parenting or more family conversations about education and goals, the odds of a young person being the first generation to attend some-college increase by about a fifth, and those of attending a four-year college increase by a third to half.

In their own words:
Sharing conversations about education and goals
from a White female from the West

My Mom and I would always have conversations like, "What do you want to be when you grow up?" When I was really little it was just how you talk to little kids. I was actually just talking to my Mom about this recently: when I was really little and taking piano lessons I wanted to be the person in the department store who played the piano. The Nordstrom piano player. It sounded really nice. That's what I wanted to do.

Then when I got older, like middle school, that's the first time I remember talking to my Mom about college. My Mom took me on this trip up the east coast. My Mom was always trying to take me on trips and save up so we could go somewhere together. So we went on one of those packaged bus tours up the east coast cities.

One of the places we went on the trip was Colonial Williamsburg, which I ate up with a spoon. We were learning about US history in school, and I was the hugest dork about history when I was a kid. I read, like, every historical novel about US history in the public library. I was really into it. And there's also a college right there, and at the time I was like, "Perfect! I will go to college here so I can work in Colonial Williamsburg!" That was my plan. And my Mom was like, "Yeah, that would be great! You should come here and go to college! You should go for it!"

My parents were always cheering me on. They wanted to have those conversations with me. Especially my Mom. She was always the one who was like, "Yeah, you should totally do that!"

- Responsive *and* directive parenting and greater parent involvement also increase the odds of a young person being the first generation to obtain a four-year college education by about a third.

In their own words:
The value of involved parenting
from a Hispanic female from the West

My parents definitely knew my friends. It's a small town, so everyone knows each other. They definitely knew my friends and their families. It was mostly like, maybe our parents would talk while they were in the parking lot picking us up. And I have a particular friend who I've kept in touch with even now that I'm at college, and I think our families are somewhat closer than any of my other friends' families.

In high school my Mom started to get to know more of my teachers too. Whenever I went to a major competition we had a tamale sale to raise funds, and that's how I think a lot of the teachers got to know her. We used the school kitchen in one of the classrooms. It was me, my Mom, and a few other students raising the funds to go. We sold about a thousand tamales. I think the first year maybe it was only six hundred, that year we were able to make them in one day. The second year it was a thousand-and-some so we had to do it in two days. Me and my Mom, we were there both of those days. And then we'd have some student volunteers who would come help out. That's how some of my teachers got to know my Mom.

Also my career counselor, I became super close with her, and she became super close with my Mom too. She genuinely wanted to help me, and proofread my essays, and she actually went with me to my first major competition. She wanted to get to know my

> *parents so my parents would feel comfortable having her go with me. And so my parents invited her for dinner, and we've stayed in touch with her. When I'm home from college, sometimes she'll stop by and say hi. She definitely had a relationship with our family.*

- Interaction styles also exert a powerful role in families with a history of going to college. This is true for college legacies who replicate their parents' college attainment; for these youth strong family relationships can be an enormous support. Valuable family relationships also protect against downward mobility. That is, when highly educated families do *not* share supportive relationships, their children are less likely to replicate their parents' higher education. Once again, nonmaterial resources—family relationships—can help children thrive regardless of a family's socioeconomic level.

> ***In their own words:***
> ***Parents protect kids' achievements***
> *from a White female from the West*
>
> *My Mom was the one who laid down the law. She wanted to know who I was out with. I didn't have an explicit curfew, but she wanted to know who I was going to be with and when I was coming home. And I knew she would still be awake when I came home, or she'd wake up, she's a really light sleeper. I would go check in with her before I went to bed. She was along those lines.*
>
> *When I got to high school if there were people I was hanging out with who she didn't like she'd let me know. Like, in high school all my friends did theater. I kind of wanted to do theater with them too but it took a lot of time. Particularly when it got*

close to a show, the week ahead of time or the two weeks ahead of time were like 24-7 doing theater.

I don't remember them explicitly saying this, but a lot of the theater kids started drinking and doing drugs and my parents could tell that some of these kids were maybe not a great influence. My parents were just like, "You don't need to be hanging out with these people." Which in retrospect I think was probably wise. At the time I resented it but in retrospect they were right.

My Mom told me, "No, I don't want you doing that, it takes too much time." Instead, I ended up helping with the stage crew. I could go once a week to do it, I didn't have to be there every day. And I could still hang out with my friends and help out with the show, but it wasn't in such an intensive role. It struck a balance.

IMPLICATIONS

This book is directed in large part toward families with children whom they hope will go to college—which is to say, the vast majority of American families. It points to valuable family relationships as a defining feature of an educationally successful adolescence. It is brimming with analyses that provide clues to how families can support their children's educations, regardless of their socioeconomic level, and first-hand stories from first-generation students about exactly how their families supported their achievements.

However, there are other implications as well. Perhaps most important, these findings offer useful information for affecting public policies. While parent education and family income are generally relatively well established at a child's birth, parent-child relationships are just beginning. Further, they are malleable: beneficial behaviors can be encouraged and cultivated across childhood, for the eighteen or so years leading to high school graduation. There are a number of ways that the institutions in our communities can provide information to parents about the options before them that can support their ambitions to see their children go to college.

One venue for implementing productive policies is high schools. While families and schools have traditionally been seen as separate spheres, programs that bridge the gap between school and family influences on academic achievement have already reaped promising rewards. Beth Simon (2004) found that the more high schools contact parents about their children's courses, planned courses, and postsecondary plans, the more parents talk with their children about school and college planning, work with their children on homework, and attend college-planning workshops. When schools reach out to parents about *how* to help their children with homework, parents more often help with school projects and homework. Similarly, Steven Sheldon and Joyce Epstein (2005) showed that school communications about opportunities to volunteer prompt parents to more frequently talk with their children about academic issues. Thus, supportive family relationships offer actionable levers, which may be developed through specific school policies and programs, designed to facilitate parental inclusion in their children's educations.

The influence of schools includes communication among parents, teachers, administrators, and counselors. Too often there are stories about how certain students are channeled into certain paths based on preconceived notions about their ability or potential. Counselors who know how to help parents further the potential of their children can become powerful aids to both parents and teachers in conveying such information. Likewise, administrators can structure school goals, course options, teacher training, and school schedules to lead students to achieve their goals. For example:

- School goals can be set for the proportion of each cohort (i.e., class) to go to college, with progress tracked across years.

- More courses that qualify for college admissions requirements can be included in the schedule, as well as more Advanced Placement (AP) and Honors courses, and more students can be encouraged to take them.

- Lower-track courses in given subjects can be reduced or eliminated from the school schedule.

- Teachers can be trained in how to work with a broader cross-section of students to meet higher standards and goals.

- Schedules can be modified to expand college-access courses and supports, such as through early morning or late afternoon offerings, Saturday classes, and more extra curricular activities.

- Students can be encouraged to take the PSAT/MNSQT as high school sophomores, and guided towards online and in-person tutoring to improve their success on these tests.

With regard to first-generation college going, Michael Hout (2011) as well as Jennie Brand and Yu Xie (2010) have demonstrated that a college education contributes greater benefits to children with low odds of college attendance than to those most likely to pursue college. This means the children of less-educated parents have the most to gain. It also means that interventions targeted toward lower socioeconomic status families may contribute the biggest gains, opening the doors of higher education to increasing numbers. Here again, schools can play a key role by organizing more school-parent connections. Examples:

- Back-to-school meetings for parents in the fall each year, held in the evening when they are more likely to be free of work responsibilities.

- Meetings between parents and school counselors, both to convey the value of higher education and help plan children's future course selections.

- More frequent and complete reports to parents regarding their children's progress, via paper and/or electronic reports (i.e., school-to-home e-communication).

- Social activities involving parents and their children such as school tours, receptions, picnics, and potluck meals.

- Celebratory events at the end of reporting periods, semesters, and school years to honor children's achievements, with rewards for various kinds of achievements (e.g., attendance, GPA improvements, individual course excellence).

- Information about the college application process, including deadlines, and possible test and application fee waivers for low-income families.

- Information about the cost of various college paths, as well as the various forms of support, such as scholarships, fellowships, and work-study programs, to correct misconceptions about the unaffordability of college.

- Information about programs specifically designed to support first-generation or at-risk students in pursuing college, such as AVID, CollegeEd, QuestBridge, summer bridge programs, Talent Search, and Upward Bound.

Countless community channels are also available for reaching families, such as:

- Public libraries
- Churches
- Social service agencies
- Community clubs and organizations

In general, strengthening the bond between schools and families can help to level the playing field for youth from low SES families.

Another implication of these findings relates to our economy. Understanding what distinguishes educationally mobile students is of particular importance at a time when increasing numbers of American jobs rely on an educated workforce to support our role in the global economy. While preparing all students for "college and career" has become a national goal, the more we can help guide young people in directions that will prove rewarding and fulfilling for them the better. *Some* education beyond high school is necessary for the majority of interesting, meaningful, and valuable work. Thus helping virtually all students toward the best college option for them is consonant with strengthening our national economy.

Again, high schools can play a key role. Since many youth have only a vague sense for the postsecondary options awaiting them, high schools can provide more extensive counseling, and even brief classes, detailing these options and the pros and cons of each. Among such options are:

- GED programs for students who have dropped out of high school or are about to.

- Apprenticeships, in which graduating seniors receive formal classroom and on-the-job training in a trade, often leading to a license and journeyman status.

- Dual enrollment options, which offer courses for high school students (taught either at the high school or a nearby community college) that fulfill credit at both levels, giving students a head start on college.

- Community college career-related programs, from one or a few courses to a sequence leading to a certificate in some field. This can be a meaningful form of job preparation leading to improved careers.

- A two-year Associates of Arts (AA) degree, useful as an outcome in itself, or a less-expensive means of completing the first two years of a four-year degree. Many states provide an easy transfer system for such two-year graduates to enter their four-year public colleges.

- The wide variety of four-year options, from

relatively inexpensive and broad-access public colleges, to more selective public universities with graduate programs, to private colleges and universities across a range of selectivity and cost.

Students can be encouraged to visit colleges to gain a first hand sense for where they may apply. High schools can organize field trips to nearby colleges, and help students organize independent visits to colleges farther afield. Students can attend college fairs and information nights and weekends. For their part, colleges can work to offer more such opportunities, coordinating with local high schools to be sure a broad range of students are made aware of such opportunities. Professors can serve as mentors, offer free lectures during prospective student/parent days or weekends, and coordinate with high school teachers in their field to promote sensible sequences of courses from high school through college. Admissions offices can provide materials to help ease the application process, and financial aid staff can explain the range of support available to students from lower income families, the qualifications for such aid, and how to go about applying for it.

These kinds of first hand interactions make a big difference, particularly for first-generation students, as one described:

In their own words:
Choosing a college
from a White male from the West

In high school I went over to a friend's house on New Years Eve, and a guy who had graduated probably the year before came over too, and he had on a college sweatshirt. I didn't know the school, but he told me it was the college where he was going and I thought, "Well that sounds good to me." So that became one of the four schools that I applied to.

My girlfriend and I drove up to the school and looked around campus. It looked like a college campus with brick and ivy and all that stuff, and so

> *I said, "Okay, this is it!" And that's how I ended up there.*

Additionally, students should be made aware of college campus support systems available to first-generation students, or any student needing support. They may also be pointed towards all of the resources they're entitled to as students, such as libraries, tutoring, study groups, and online resources—all at no additional cost once enrolled.

Another way in which high schools and the communities in which they reside can contribute to student success is by forming school-business partnerships in which local employers help to inform and support young people's educations and career options. The more young people understand the career options that lie in their possible futures, and the importance of more education for higher level and more rewarding careers, the more seriously they are likely to view their high school preparation. First-generation students in particular may be less aware of how much education different careers require—or the variation within a field, such as the difference between becoming a medical assistant versus a doctor. Who better to help inform them of the options in their community and the kind of education needed for various positions than employers and individuals who pursued careers aligned with their interests? Examples of activities that schools and employers can cooperate in:

- Speakers from local employers who explain the kinds of products and services they provide and the training needed for various levels and positions.

- Field trips to such places of employment, with tours of the work settings and interviews with employees.

- Job shadowing, in which students spend a few hours working under someone in a local company to get a feel for the work and environment.

- Mentorships in which employees volunteer as career-related advisors, either in face-to-face meetings or via email, to students expressing an interest in their field of work.

- Internships, either paid or not, usually with high school juniors or seniors, in which students work over some period of time in a company under the guidance of a supervisor, often over the summer.

- Scholarships, in which employers provide financial help to graduating seniors, often those interested in the field in which the employer works, with the possibility of a job once they complete their training.

Future research

The findings here can also be useful for informing further research. To begin, the importance of family relationships for educational attainment identifies some of what is often described as "unobserved heterogeneity" in studies of educational attainment. What is "unobserved heterogeneity"? It is the variations in data that couldn't be explained through whatever the particular study was examining. Well, now we can explain at least some of them, such as how families with different structural characteristics promote certain attainments, and why there is variation in those attainments. Future research can build on the findings here—family relationships may help to explain much of the unexplained variation in youth's outcomes.

Likewise, future research can examine how to strengthen the findings here. Perhaps the largest limitation of the book is the one mentioned up front: it analyzes *observational* data. This isn't *causal* research, so I can't be sure that family relationships are truly the driving force supporting children's higher educational achievements. As you now know, youth who make it to college—whether or not their parents did—are far more likely to share supportive family relationships than those who don't, and these family relationships powerfully predict educational success even when controlling statistically for all sorts of factors that are likely to affect such success. But social effects are so complex that even if you control for a dozen variables, you can't be *certain* there isn't a thirteenth one that was not yet considered that plays a role.

The gold standard in social research for proving that one variable causes another is a randomized study. What does that mean? Here's an example: Let's say there's a new after-school program where youth are having great outcomes, but you want to *prove* that the program is what's making the difference. What do you do? Invite families to apply, and randomly select just half of them for a slot. Then follow *all* of these families over time to see whether students who participate in the program do better. If they do, then you can be sure it's the program that made the difference. If they don't, it's probably something about the kinds of families that apply to such programs that explains the difference. Maybe these are particularly supportive families, always on the lookout for opportunities for their kids, so if they don't get randomly admitted to one program they'll look for another, or engage with their kids in valuable ways on their own.

The problem for researchers is that we're talking about *families* here, and randomization of families isn't an option. No one can arbitrarily assign children to more or less supportive families, follow them across childhood, and see whether those who lived with more supportive parents did better.

That said, it *would* be possible to randomly assign children and their parents to programs designed to *foster* supportive family relationships. Any number of programs have been found to be effective in cultivating supportive relationships. If children assigned by lottery to such programs were more often upwardly mobile and less often downwardly mobile than children who (by lottery) did not participate in such programs, these findings would have strong causal grounds. This would be an exciting future study.

Another promising direction for future research would be to directly analyze the role of income alongside family relationships in shaping children's intergenerational educational paths. All of the original analyses in this book control for family income, meaning that findings identify the effects of family relationships across the economic spectrum. But it's worth remembering that while first-generation students, on average, have less money than those with college-educated parents, they also tend to have higher family incomes than the youth who replicate parents' no-college paths. So, while findings herein hold for families up and down the socioeconomic spectrum, it would be interesting for future research to examine the effects of economics on intergenerational educational trajectories, controlling for supportive family interactions.

While awaiting such studies, let's celebrate what has been learned. We've learned that a substantial proportion of socioeconomically disadvantaged youth *invested with supportive family relationships* manage to rise above the educational achievements of their parents, while a substantial proportion of advantaged youth *deprived of supportive family relationships* fall short of their parents' higher education achievements. In short, across the board, family relationships predict intergenerational educational trajectories. While we suspected this before, and had some good initial clues from previous studies, we now have a substantial body of nationally representative and statistically significant data to confirm it, and to illustrate the many ways in which such supportive relationships operate. My hope is that this can be of use to families across America.

In conclusion, here is one final quote from a young person—a quote that illustrates the motivation to write this book:

In their own words:
I want to tell my parents
from a White female from the West

I want to tell my parents that I'm helping you with this book. Because I think my Mom always feels like, "I couldn't help you with your homework, I couldn't help you figure out what to do in college," because they didn't have the experience.

I want to tell them that without their emotional support, I couldn't have done it. Parents can be such a resource for resilience. Parents should know that—parents who read your book should hear that: I wouldn't have gone to college without my parents' encouragement and support.

References

Aaronson D. 1998. Using sibling data to estimate the impact of neighborhoods on children's educational outcomes. *J. Hum. Resour.* 33:915–46

Ainsworth JW. 2002. Why does it take a village? The mediation of neighborhood effects on educational achievement. *Soc. Forces* 81(1)117–52

American Human Development Project. 2009. *Goals for the common good: Exploring the impact of education.* Accessed March 2015: http://www.measureofamerica.org/file/common_good_forecaster_full_report.pdf

Arum R, Roksa J. 2011. *Academically Adrift: Limited learning on college campuses*. University of Chicago Press. Chicago.

Association of American Colleges and Universities. 2005. *Liberal education outcomes: A preliminary report on student achievement in college.* Accessed March 2015: http://www.aacu.org/advocacy/pdfs/LEAP_Report_FINAL.pdf

Astone N, McLanahan S. 1991. Family structure, parental practices and high school completion. *American Sociological Review* 56: 309-320

Astone NM, Nathanson CA, Schoen R, Kim YJ. 1999. Family demography, social theory, and investment in social capital. *Population and Development Review* 25(1):1-31

Bae Y, Choy S, Geddes C, Sable J, Snyder T. 2000. *Trends in educational equity of girls and women.* Washington, DC: National Center for Education Statistics, Department of Education

Bandura A, Barbaranelli C, Caprara GV, Pastorelli C. 1996. Multifaceted impact of self-efficacy beliefs on academic functioning. *Child Development* 67:1206–1222

Baker TL, Velez W. 1996. Access to and opportunity in postsecondary education in the United States: A review. *Sociology of Education.* 69:82-101

Barr C. 2015. *Impact of Student Loan Debt on Young People.* Debt.org. Accessed March 2015 at http://www.debt.org/students/

Baum S, Ma J, Payea K. 2010. *Education pays: The benefits of higher education for individuals and society.* Trends in Higher Education Series, Report No. 7. Accessed March 2015: http://trends.collegeboard.org/sites/default/files/education-pays-2010-full-report.pdf

Bernick M. April 10, 2014. *It Doesn't Matter Where you go to College.* Time. Accessed March 2015: http://time.com/54342/it-doesnt-matter-where-you-go-to-college/

Bourdieu P, Passeron C. 1973. *Cultural Reproduction and Social Reproduction.* In Richard K. Brown (Ed.), Knowledge, Education and Cultural Change. London: Tavistock.

Bound J, Lovenheim M, Turner SE. 2007. *Understanding the decrease in college completion rates and the increased time to the Baccalaureate degree.* PSC Research Report No. 07-626. Population Studies Center, University of Michigan

Bozick R. 2007. Making it through the first year of college: The role of students' economic resources, employment, and living arrangements. *Sociology of Education.* 80(3):261-85

Brand JE, Xie Y. 2010. Who benefits most from college? Evidence for negative selection in heterogeneous economic returns to higher education. *American Sociological Review.* 75(2):273-302

Brooks-Gunn J, Duncan GJ, Aber JL, eds. 1997a. *Neighborhood Poverty*: Vol. I: *Context and Consequences for Children.* New York: Russell Sage Foundation

Brooks-Gunn J, Duncan GJ, Aber JL, eds. 1997b. *Neighborhood Poverty:* Vol. II: *Policy Implications in Studying Neighborhoods.* New York: Russell Sage Foundation

Brooks-Gunn J, Duncan GJ, Klebanov PK, Sealand N. 1993.Doneighborhoods influence child and adolescent development? *Am. J. Sociol.* 99(2):353–95

Bruni F. Where You Go Is Not Who You'll Be. An Antidote to the College Admissions Mania. 2015. Hachette Book Group. https://www.hachettebookgroup.com/...you-go-is-not-who-youll.../9781455532704/

Buchmann C, Dalton D. 2002. Interpersonal influences and education aspirations in 12 countries: The importance of institutional context. *Sociology of Education* 75(2): 99–122

Bureau of Labor Statistics, Current Population Survey, U.S. Department of Labor, March 2014.

Bureau of Labor Statistics, Current Population Survey. Unemployment rate and earnings by educational attainment, 2013: http://www.bls.gov/careeroutlook/2014/data-on-display/education-still-pays.htm

Bureau of Labor Statistics, U.S. Department of Labor, News Release. *Employment Projections—2012-2011.* Accessed March 2015 at http://www.bls.gov/news.release/pdf/ecopro.pdf.

Burtless G. 1996. *Does Money Matter? The Effect of School Resources on Student Achievement and Adult Success.* Washington, DC: Brookings Inst. Press

Carbonaro WJ. 1998. A little help from my friends' parents: Intergenerational closure and educational outcomes. *Sociology of Education* 71:295–313

Card D, Krueger AB. 1992. Does school quality matter? Returns to education and the characteristics of public schools in the United States. *J. Polit. Econ.* 100(1):1–40

Card D, Rothstein J. 2007. Racial segregation and the black-white test score gap. *J. Public Econ.* 91(11–12):2158–84

Carnevale AP, Rose SJ, Cheah B. 2009. *The College Payoff: Education, Occupations, Lifetime Earnings.* The Georgetown University Center on Education and the Workforce

Case A, Katz LF. 1991. *The company you keep: the effects of family and neighborhood on disadvantaged youths.* NBER Work. Pap. W3705, Natl. Bur. Econ. Res., Cambridge, MA

Casselman B. September 12, 2014. *The Economic Guide to Picking a College Major.* Higher Ed: FiveThirtyEight. Accessed March 2015: http://fivethirtyeight.com/features/the-economic-guide-to-picking-a-college-major/#fn-1

Choy S. 2001. Students whose parents did not go to college: Postsecondary access, persistence, and attainment. *Findings from the Condition of Education*, a report from the National Center for Education Statistics

Clotfelter CT, Ladd HF, Vigdor JL. 2007. *How and why do teacher credentials matter for student achievement?* NBERWork. Pap. W12828, Natl. Bur. Econ. Res., Cambridge, MA

Coleman J. 1990. *Equality and Achievement in Education.* Boulder, CO: Westview Press

Coleman, J. 1988. Social Capital in the Creation of Human Capital. *The American Journal of Sociology*, Supplement:

Organizations and Institutions: Sociological and Economic Approaches to the Analysis of Social Structure. 94:S95-S120

Coleman J. 1987. Families and schools. *American Educational Research Association.* 16(6):32-8

Coleman J, Hoffer T, Kilgore S. 1981. *Public and private schools.* Washington, D.C.: National Center for Education Statistics

Coleman JS, Campbell EQ, Hobson CJ, McPartland J, Mood AM, Weinfeld RD, York RL. 1966. *Equality of Educational Opportunity.* Washington, DC: U.S. Government Printing Office

College Board, Trends in College Pricing (2013). Figure 4 (p14) "Average Annual Percentage Increases in Inflation-Adjusted Published Prices by Decade" 1983-84 to 2013-14: http://trends.collegeboard.org/sites/default/files/college-pricing-2013-full-report.pdf

CollegeBoard. *First-Generation students: Counseling first-generation students about college.* Accessed September 2015: https://professionals.collegeboard.com/guidance/prepare/first-generation

Conference Board, The. 2006. Corporate Voices for Working Families, the Partnership for 21st Century Skills, and the society of Human Resource Management. *Are they really ready to work?* Employers' perspectives on the basic knowledge and applied skills of new entrants to the 21st century US workforce.

Connell J, Halpern-Fisher B. 1997. *How neighborhoods affect educational outcomes in middle childhood and adolescence*. See Brooks-Gunn et al. 1997a, pp. 174–99

Crane J. 1991. The epidemic theory of ghettos and neighborhood effects on dropping out and teenage childbearing. *Am. J. Sociol.* 96:1226–60

Crosnoe R, Mistry RS, Elder GH. 2002. Economic disadvantage, family dynamics, and adolescent enrollment in higher education. *Journal of Marriage and the Family*. 64(3):690-702

Crowder K, South SJ. 2003. Neighborhood distress and school dropout: the variable significance of community context. *Soc. Sci. Res.* 32(4):659–98

D. Hart Research Associates. 2008. *How should colleges assess and improve student learning? Employers' views on the accountability challenge*. A survey of employers conducted on behalf of The Association of American Colleges and Universities

Dale SB, Kreuger AB. November 2002. *Estimating the Payoff to Attending a More Selective College: An Application of Selection on Observables and Unobservables.* The Quarterly Journal of Economics

Dayton E. 2012. "First in my Family": Family relationships and educational mobility. Doctoral dissertation. Johns Hopkins University. Baltimore, MD

DeLuca S. 2007. Late bloomers and fade-outs: Does the timing of school performance matter in the long run? Manuscript currently under review

DeLuca S, Dayton E. 2009. Switching Social Contexts: The Effects of Housing Mobility and School Choice Programs on Youth Outcomes. *Annual Review of Sociology*. 35:457-91

DeLuca S, Rosenbaum JE. 2001. Individual agency and the life course: Do low SES students get less long-term pay-off for their school efforts? *Sociological Focus*. 34, 357-376

Demographics of the United States. Accessed May 2015 from: http://en.wikipedia.org/wiki/Demographics_of_the_United_States

Dennis JM, Phinney JS, Chuateco LI. 2005. The role of motivation, parental support, and peer support in the academic success of ethnic minority first-generation college students. *Journal of College Student Development.* 46(3):223-236

Downey DB, von Hippel PT, Broh BA. 2004. Are schools the great equalizer? Cognitive inequality during the summer months and the school year. *Am. Sociol. Rev.* 69:613–35

Dunifon R, Duncan GJ, Brooks-Gunn J. 2001. *As ye sweep, so shall ye reap.* AEA Papers and Proceedings, The Benefits of Skill. 91(2):150-154

Eagly AH, Ashmore RD, Makhijani MG, Longo LC. What Is Beautiful Is Good, but: A Meta-analytic Review of Research on the Physical Attractiveness Stereotype. *Psychological Bulletin.* 1991;110(1):109–128

Elder GH, Eccles JS, Ardelt M, Lord S. 1995. Inner-city parents under economic pressure: Perspectives on the strategies of parenting. *Journal of Marriage and the Family.* 57(3):771-784

Elliott DS, Wilson WJ, Huizinga D, Sampson RJ, Elliott A, Rankin B. 1996. The effects of neighborhood disadvantage on adolescent development. *J. Res. Crime Delinq.* 33:389–426

Ensminger ME, Lamkin RP, Jacobson N. 1996. School leaving: a longitudinal perspective including neighborhood effects. *Child Dev.* 67(5):2400–16

Entwisle DR, Alexander KL, Oleson LS. 1997. *Children, Schools, and Inequality*. Boulder, CO: Westview

Fan X, Chen M. 2001. Parental involvement and students' academic achievement: A meta- analysis. *Educational Psychology Review* 13(1): 1–22

Farkas G, Grobe RP, Shehan D, Shuan Y. 1990. Cultural resources and school success: Gender, ethnicity, and poverty groups within an urban school district. *American Sociological Review* 55:127-142

Feingold A. Good-looking people are not what we think. *Psychological Bulletin.*1992;111:304–341

Ferguson RF, Ladd HF. 1996. How and why money matters: an analysis of Alabama schools. See Ladd 1996, pp. 265–98

Finn JD. 1993. *School engagement and students at risk.* Buffalo, NY: U.S. Department of Education, National Center for Educational Statistics

Furstenberg FF, Cook T, Eccles J, Elder GH. 1999. *Managing to Make It: Urban Families in High-Risk Neighborhoods*. Chicago: Univ. Chicago Press

Garner CL, Raudenbush SW. 1991. Neighborhood effects on educational attainment: a multilevel analysis. *Sociol. Educ.* 64:251–62

Gofen A. 2007. *Family capital: How first-generation higher-education students break the intergenerational cycle*. Working paper with the Institute for Research on Poverty at the University of Wisconsin-Madison

Goldrick-Rab S. 2006. Following their every move: An investigation of social-class differences in college pathways. *Sociology of Education*. 79:61-79

Goyette K, Xie Y. 1999. Educational expectations of Asian Americans youths: Determinants and ethnic differences. *Sociology of Education*. 72(1):22-36

Greenberger E, Chen C. 1996. Perceived family relationships and depressed mood in early and late adolescence: A comparison of European and Asian Americans. *Developmental Psychology*. 32(4):707-16

Hagan J, MacMillan R, Wheaton B. 1996. New did in town: Social capital and the life course effects of family migration on children. *American Sociological Review* 61: 368-385

Hanson SL. 1994. Lost talent: Unrealized educational aspirations and expectations among U.S. youths. *Sociology of Education* 67(3):159–183

Hanushek EA, Rivkin SG. 2006. *School quality and the black-white test achievement gap*.NBERWork. Pap. 12651, Natl. Bur. Econ. Res., Cambridge, MA

Hao L, Bonstead-Bruns M. 1998. Parent-child differences in educational expectations and the academic achievement of immigrant and native students. *Sociology of Education.* 71:175–198

Haveman R, Wolfe B. 1994. *Succeeding generations: On the effects of investments in children.* New York: Russell Sage Foundation

Henderson AT, Berla N. 1994. *A new generation of evidence: The family is critical to student achievement.* Washington, DC: National Committee for Citizens in Education

Hershbein B, Kearney. September 2014. *Major Decisions: What Graduates Earn over their Lifetimes.* The Hamilton Project. Accessed March 2015: http://www.hamiltonproject.org/papers/major_decisions_what_graduates_earn_over_their_lifetimes/

Holzer HJ. 1991. The spatial mismatch hypothesis: what has the evidence shown? *Urban Stud.* 28:105–22

Horn L, Nunez AM. 2000. *Mapping the road to college: First-generation students' math track, planning strategies, and context of support.* Statistical Analysis Report, Postsecondary Education Descriptive Analysis Reports, from the National Center for Education Statistics.

Hout M. 2011. Social and economic returns to college education in the United States. *Annual. Review of Sociology.* 37

Hout M. 2008. Rationing Opportunity: The role of America's colleges and Universities in Graduation Trends. *University of California, Berkeley, Survey Research Center.* Working paper.

Ihlanfeldt KR, Sjoquist DL. 1998. The spatial mismatch hypothesis: a review of recent studies and their implications for welfare reform. *Hous. Policy Debate* 9(4):849–92

Ishitani TT. 2003. A longitudinal approach to assessing attrition behavior among first- generation students: Time-varying effects of pre-college characteristics. *Research in Higher Education.* (44)4:433-449

Jarrett RL. 1997. African American family and parenting strategies in impoverished neighborhoods. *Qual. Sociol.* 20(2):275–

88
Jacob BA. 2002. Where the boys aren't: non-cognitive skills, returns to school and the gender gap in higher education. *Economics of Education Review*. 21:589-598

Jencks C, Phillips M. 1998. *The Black-White Test Score Gap*. Washington, DC: Brookings Inst. Press

King, JE. 2006. *Gender equity in higher education: 2006*. American Council on Education, Washington, DC

Kirst M. Women Earn More Degrees Than Men; Gap Keeps Increasing. Based on an article from AEI Ideas, summarized by Carnegie Foundation. The College Puzzle. Accessed April 2015 at: http://collegepuzzle.stanford.edu/?p=3131#sthash.IGj9nzrf.5nvFhOWj.dpuf

Kohn, M.L. (1966). *Class and Conformity*. Homewood IL: The Dorsey Press

Krueger A, Dale SB. 2000. Estimating the Payoff to Attending a More Selective College. National Bureau of Economic Research. https://www.princeton.edu/pr/news/00/q1/0126-krueger.htm

Langlois JH, Kalakanis L, Rubenstein AJ, Larson A, Hallam M, Smoot M. Maxims or myths of beauty? A meta-analytic and theoretical review. *Psychological Bulletin*. 2000;126:390–423

Lareau A. 2011. Unequal Childhoods: Class, Race, and Family Life, 2nd Edition with an Update a Decade Later. University of California Press

Lareau A. 2002. Invisible inequality: Social class and childrearing in black families and white families. *American Sociological Review*. 67(5):747-776

Lareau A. 1989. *Home Advantage: Social Class and Parental Intervention in Elementary Education*. New York: Falmer

Leonhardt D. *College Costs: Rising, Yet Often Exaggerated*. New York Times, August 22, 2013.

Leonhardt D. *How the Government Exaggerates the Cost of College*. New York Times, July 29, 2014. Accessed March 2015: http://www.nytimes.com/2014/07/29/upshot/how-the-government-exaggerates-the-cost-of-college.html?_r=0&abt=0002&abg=1

Lillard D. 1993. *Neighborhood effects on educational attainment*. CEH Work. Pap. RP-93-5, Cornell Univ., Ithaca, NY

Lleras C. 2006. *Do skills and behaviors in high school matter? The contribution of noncognitive factors in explaining differences in educational attainment and earnings.* Manuscript under review

Looney A, Greenstone M. October 2012. *Regardless of the cost, college still matters.* The Hamilton Project. Accessed March 2015: http://www.hamiltonproject.org/papers/regardless_of_the_cost_college_still_matters/

Lynskey M, Hall W. 2000. The effects of adolescent cannabis use on educational attainment: A review. *Addiction.* 95(11):1621-30

Madsen SR. 2012. *The Nonfinancial Benefits of Higher Education for Individuals and Society.* Utah Women and Education Initiative

MacLeod J. 1987. *Ain't No Makin It: Aspirations and Attainment in a Low-Income Neighborhood.* Boulder, CO: Westview

Madsen SR. 2012. *The non-financial returns on investing in higher education for individuals and society.* Utah Women's Education Initiative, WICHE Commission Meeting, University of Utah, SLC, Utah

Martin A, Lehren A. May 12, 2012. *Degrees of Debt: A generation hobbled by the soaring cost of college.* New York Times. Accessed March 2015: http://www.nytimes.com/2012/05/13/business/student-loans-weighing-down-a-generation-with-heavy-debt.html?pagewanted=all

Mayer SE, Peterson PE, eds. 1999. *Earning and Learning: How Schools Matter.* Washington, DC: Brookings Inst. Press

McCarron GP, Inkelas KK. 2006. The gap between educational aspirations and attainment for first-generation college students and the role of parental involvement. *Journal of College Student Development.* 47(5):534-549

McLafferty S, Preston V. 1992. Spatial mismatch and labor market segmentation for African-American and Latina women. *Econ. Geogr.* 68:406–31

McLanahan S, Sandefur G. 1994. *Growing up with a single parent: What hurts, what helps.* Cambridge, MA: Harvard University Press

McNeal RB. 1999. Parent involvement as social capital: Differential effectiveness on science achievement, truancy, and dropping out. *Social Forces.*78:117–144

Miech R, Essex MJ, Goldsmith HH. 2001. Socioeconomic status and the adjustment to school: The role of self-regulation during early childhood. *Sociology of Education* 74:102-120

Morgan SL. 2005. *On the Edge of Commitment: Educational Attainment and Race in the United States*. Stanford University Press.

National Center for Education Statistics (NCES). 2010. *Descriptive Summary of 2003-2004 Beginning Postsecondary Students: After six years*. Washington, DC: US Department of Education

National Center for Education Statistics (NCES), National Postsecondary Student Aid Study (NPSAS). Accessed March 2015: http://nces.ed.gov/surveys/npsas/

National Center for Education Statistics (NCES). 2014. Undergraduate enrollment. Accessed April 2015: https://nces.ed.gov/programs/coe/indicator_cha.asp

Nye B, Hedges LV, Konstantopoulos S. 1999. The long-term effects of small classes: a five-year follow-up of the Tennessee class size experiment. *Educ. Eval. Policy Anal.* 21:127–42

Odland S. 2012. *College costs out of control*. Forbes. Accessed January 7, 2015 from: http://www.forbes.com/sites/steveodland/2012/03/24/college-costs-are-soaring/

Pascarella ET, Pierson CT, Wolniak GC, Terenzini PT. 2004. First-generation college students: Additional evidence on college experiences and outcomes. *The Journal of Higher Education*. 75(3):249-284

Pascarella ET, Terenzini PT. 1998. Studying college students in the 21st century: Meeting new challenges. *The Review of Higher Education*. 21(2):151-165

Pascarella ET, Terenzini PT. 2005. *How college affects students: A third decade of research.* San Francisco: Jossey-Bass.

Pearlin LI, Menaghan EG, Lieberman MA, Mullan JT. 1981. The stress process. *Journal of Health and Social Behavior*. 22:337-356

Pew Research Center, Social & Demographic Trends. February 2014. *The rising cost of not going to college.* Accessed January 7, 2015 at http://www.pewsocialtrends.org/2014/02/11/the-rising-cost-of-not-going-to-college/

Phinney JS, Haas K. 2003. The process of coping among ethnic minority first generation college freshmen: A narrative approach. *The Journal of Social Psychology*, 143(6), 707-726.

Portes A. 1998. Social capital: Its origins and applications in modern sociology. *Annual Review of Sociology.* 24:1-24

Putnam R. 200X. *Social capital: Measurement and consequences.* Kennedy School of Government, Harvard University.

Raley S, Suzanne B. Sons, daughters, and family processes: Does Gender of children matter? *Annu. Rev. Sociol.* 2006. 32:401–21

Rau W, Durand A. 2000. The academic ethic and college grades: Does hard work help students to 'make the grade'. *Sociology of Education.* 73:19-38

Rivkin SG, Hanushek EA, Kain JF. 2005.Teachers, schools and academic achievement. *Econometrica* 73:417–58

Rosenbaum JE, DeLuca S, Miller S. 2000. *Are non-cognitive behaviors in school related to later life outcomes?* Paper presented at the Annual Meeting of the American Sociological Association. Wash., D.C.

Rosenbaum JE, Stephan JL, Rosenbaum JE. 2010. Beyond One-Size-Fits-All College Dreams: Alternative pathways to desirable careers. *American Educator*

Sackett PR, Kuncel NR, Arneson JJ, Cooper SR, Waters SD. 2009. *Socio-economic status and the relationship between the SAT and freshman GPA: An analysis of data from 41 colleges and universities.* The College Board

Saenz VB, Hurtado S, Barrera D, Wolf D, Yeung F. 2007. *First in my family: A profile of first-generation college students at four-year institutions since 1971.* Los Angeles: Higher Education Research Institute.

Sampson RJ, Laub JH. 1990. Crime and deviance over the life course: The salience of adult social bonds. *American Sociological Review.* 55(5):609-27

Sampson RJ, Morenoff JD, Thomas GR. 2002. Assessing "neighborhood effects": social processes and new directions in research. *Annu. Rev. Sociol.* 28:443–78

Sandefur GD, Meier AM, Campbell ME. 2006. Family resources, social capital, and college attendance. *Social Science Research.* 35(2):525-553

Sandefur G, Meier A, Hernandez P. 1999. *Families, social capital, and educational continuation.* Working paper with the Center for Demography and Ecology at the University of Wisconsin-Madison

Sandefur RL, Laumann EO. 1998. A paradigm for social capital. *Rationality and Society* 10:481-501

Seccombe K. 2002. “Beating the odds” verses “changing the odds”: Poverty, resilience, and family policy. *Journal of Marriage and the Family*. 64(2):384-394

Sewell W, Hauser RM. 1980. The Wisconsin longitudinal study of social and psychological factors in aspirations and achievements. *Research in Sociology of Education* 1: 59–99

Shea J. 2000. Does parents’ money matter? *Journal of Public Economics* 77:155–184

Sheldon S, Epstein J. 2005. Involvement Counts: Family and Community Partnerships and Mathematics Achievement. *The Journal of Educational Research*. 98(4):196-207

Shouse R, Schneider B, Plank S. 1992. Teacher assessments of student effort: Effects of student characteristics and school type. *Educational Policy* 6:266-288

Simon, B. 2004. High School Outreach and Family Involvement. *Social Psychology of Education* 7:185–209

Social Security Administration, Cost-of-Living Adjustments: https://www.ssa.gov/oact/cola/colaseries.html

Simon JB, Murphy JJ, Smith SM. 2005. Understanding and fostering family resilience. *The Family Journal* 13(4): 427–436

Sullivan ML. 1989. *Getting Paid: Youth Crime and Work in the Inner City*. Ithaca, NY: Cornell Univ. Press

Taylor P, Fry R, Oates R. The Rising Costs of Not Going to College. 2014. Pew Research Center. www.pewsocialtrends.org/files/2014/02/SDT-higher-ed-FINAL-02-11-2014.pdf

Teachman J, Paasch K, Carver K. 1997. Social capital and the generation of human capital. *Social Forces*. 75:1343-1359

Trusty J, Niles SG. 2004. Realized potential or lost talent: High school variables and bachelor’s degree completion. *The Career Development Quarterly*. 53:2-15

Trusty J. 1998. Family influences on educational expectations of late adolescents. *The Journal of Educational Research*. 91(5):260-270

Tucker CJ, Marx J, Long L. 1998.‘Moving on’: Residential mobility and children’s school lives. *Sociology of Education* 71: 111-129

U.S. Census Bureau. 2005. *College degree nearly doubles annual earnings*, Census Bureau Reports. Accessed May 12, 2009 from: http://www.census.gov/Press-

Release/www/releases/archives/education/004214.html

U.S. Census Bureau. 2012. *Educational Attainment in the United States: 2009*. Population Characteristics. See http://www.census.gov/prod/2012pubs/p20-566.pdf

U.S. Department of Education, 2011-2012 National Postsecondary Student Aid Study. 2013. nces.ed.gov/pubs2013/2013165.pdf

U.S. Department of Education. 2006. *A Test of Leaderships: Charting the future of US Higher Educatio*n. A report of the Commission Appointed by Secretary of Education Margaret Spellings. http://www2.ed.gov/about/bdscomm/list/hiedfuture/reports/pre-pub-report.pdf

Weissmann J. May 17, 2012. *Does it Matter Where you go to College?* The Atlantic. Accessed March 2015: http://www.theatlantic.com/business/archive/2012/05/does-it-matter-where-you-go-to-college/257227/

Wirt J, Choy S, Gruner A, Sable J, Tobin R, Bae Y et al. (2000). *The condition of education 2000.* Washington, DC: U.S. Government Printing Office

White KR. 1982. The relation between socioeconomic status and academic achievement. *Psychological Bulletin.* 91(3):461-81

Zebrowitz LA, Hall JA, Murphy NA, Rhodes G. Looking smart and looking good: Facial cues to intelligence and their origins. *Personality and Social Psychology* Bulletin. 2002;28:238–249

Zebrowitz LA, Rhodes G. Sensitivity to "Bad Genes" and the Anomalous Face Overgeneralization Effect: Cue Validity, Cue Utilization, and Accuracy in Judging Intelligence and Health. *Journal of Nonverbal Behavior*. 2004;28:167–185

Zebrowitz LA. *Reading faces: Window to the soul?* Boulder, Colo.: Westview Press; 1997

Zhan M, Sherraden M. 2010. *Assets and liabilities, race/ethnicity, and children's college education.* The Center for Social Development George Warren Brown School of Social Work

Appendix

Data Source

The National Longitudinal Survey of Youth 1997 (NLSY97) provides longitudinal coverage of youth's and parents' attitudes, experiences, characteristics, and educational attainment. Sponsored by the U.S. Bureau of Labor Statistics, the NLSY97 is a nationally representative survey of youth who were ages 12 to 16 on December 31, 1996. Youth and their parents have been interviewed annually since. Initially, 147 primary sampling units (i.e., non-overlapping metropolitan areas or—within these areas—single counties or groups of counties) were drawn on to screen a total of 75,291 households to identify youth eligible for the survey. A sample of 8,984 youth living in 6,819 households was assembled, including an oversample of 2,236 Black and Hispanic youth.

Most measures in the NLSY97 are self-reported from annual personal interviews. Computer-assisted personal interview (CAPI) technology was used to lower the likelihood of collecting inconsistent data (as compared to paper-and-pencil interviews—for example, when youth provide inconsistent responses across the survey, CAPI technology prompts them to verify the correct information).

By design, the 13 and 14 year-old cohorts were asked batteries of questions that best tap into family relationships. Thus, the study analyzes these two cohorts (ages 23-24 in 2007).

The study examines both bachelor degree completers *and* other college experience (e.g., two-year college experience, or discontinued college attendance shy of a degree) to provide a multifaceted understanding of the role of family relationships in promoting various postsecondary paths.

Dependent variables

Drawing on the 13 and 14 year-old NLSY97 cohorts, the study examines (1) youth's college attendance and (2) intergenerational educational trajectories.

Youth's individual college attendance: Four-year college, any college, or no college

The study analyzes a dependent variable that includes categories for (1) four-year college students, (2) students with some-college experience, and (3) students with no college experience, using parents' college status as an independent variable.

This dependent variable was also used to create *interaction terms* between parents' college attainment and family relationships, allowing me to examine whether family relationships *mean more* in more- or less-educated families. I refer to these analyses in Chapter 6 and 8.

Table 1 • Youth's Individual College Attendance (by ages 23-24) Dependent Variable

	Children's educational status	**N**	**Sample percent**	**Weighted percent**
1. Four-year college	Four-year college enrollee or graduate	857	28 percent	32 percent
2. Some-college	Two-year college enrollee or graduate, or previously enrolled with no degree	948	31 percent	30 percent
3. No college	High school or less with no college experience	1244	40 percent	38 percent

Note: No-college students are the comparison category for all analyses.

In interpreting Table 1, note that both sample percentages and weighted percentages are presented. Because the NLSY97 oversampled Black and Hispanic youth, sample distributions do not exactly match the national distribution of youth. Therefore, to provide a clear sense for how common these educational trajectories are nationally, I also present nationally weighted distributions.

Table 1 indicates that while slightly less than a third of the sample (and weighted distribution) consists of four-year college students and some-college students respectively, about two-fifths of the sample (and weighted distribution) consists of no-college students. This distribution is similar to other sources of data, such as U.S. Census statistics.

Intergenerational educational trajectories

The study also analyzes intergenerational educational trajectories, including categories for (1) bachelors legacies, who replicate their parents' four-year college education; (2) some-college legacies, who replicate their parents' some-college education (short of a bachelors education); (3) first-generation bachelors, who attend four-year college though their parents did not; (4) first-generation some-college students, who attend some college (short of four-year college) though their parents did not; (5) downwardly mobile bachelors, who fail to replicate their parents' bachelors education; (6) downwardly mobile some-college students, who fail to replicate their parents some-college education (short of a bachelors education); and (7) no-college legacies, who replicate their parents' high school or less education. This measure allows for explicit comparisons of the effect of family relationships on intergenerational educational trajectories.

Table 2 • Intergenerational Educational Trajectories (by ages 23-24) Dependent Variable

Category	Parents	Children	N	Sample percent	Weight-ed percent
1. Bachelors college legacy	**Four-year college** ≥16 years education	**Four-year college** Four-year college continuing enrollment or graduation	459	15 percent	18 percent
2. Some-college legacy	**Some-college** 13-15 years education	**Some-college** Two-year college enrollment or graduation, or discontinued college enrollment	263	9 percent	9 percent
3. Bachelors first-generation	**No four-year college** <16 years education	**Four-year college** Four-year college continuing enrollment or graduation	398	13 percent	14 percent
4. Some-college first-generation	**No college** ≤12 years education	**Some-college** Two-year college enrollment or graduation, or discontinued college enrollment	421	14 percent	12 percent
5. Bachelors downwardly mobile	**Four-year college** ≥16 years education	**No four-year college** High school or less, some previous college, or two-year college enrollment or graduation	461	13 percent	15 percent
6. Some-college downwardly mobile	**Some-college** 13-15 years education	**No college** High school or less	255	8 percent	9 percent
7. No-college legacy	**No college** ≤12 years education	**No college** High school or less	792	26 percent	23 percent

Note: No-college legacy students are the comparison category for all analyses.

Table 2 reveals how common intergenerational educational reproduction and mobility are. About half of youth replicate their parents' education: 27 percent of the weighted distribution is composed of college legacies, with a greater proportion of youth being bachelors legacies (18 percent) than some-college legacies (9 percent). Another 23 percent of the weighted distribution is composed of no-college legacies.

However, half of youth are educationally mobile: 26 percent of the weighted distribution is composed of first-generation college students, about equally split between first-generation bachelors (14 percent) and first-generation some-college students (12 percent). The final 24 percent of the weighted distribution is composed of downwardly mobile students. Among downwardly mobile students, failing to replicate parents' bachelors' education (as 15 percent of the weighted distribution do) is more common than failing to replicate parents' some-college education (as 9 percent of the weighted distribution do).

It is worth noting that students currently enrolled in four-year colleges in 2007 (at ages 23-24) are included as four-year college students in Table 2. Only about six percent of the sample is still enrolled in four-year college in 2007 (note that when data are weighted this percentage is closer to seven percent; this is down from about ten percent in 2006 when youth were ages 22-23, and about fifteen percent in 2005 when youth were ages 21-22). However, first-generation students are twice as likely as college legacy students to be enrolled in four-year college in 2007. That is, while about four percent of the sample is comprised of first-generation students who are still enrolled, only about two percent is comprised of college legacy students who are still enrolled. While bachelors degrees are generally earned by ages 22-24 in the United States, the first-generation often takes longer, and it is important to consider the varied paths of today's students. Therefore, the small minority of youth who are still enrolled in four-year college at ages 23-24 are included as four-year college students.

It might be desirable to analyze children's educations in even more detail than this dependent variable allows, for example by including whether youth have any college experience, are enrolled in or have graduated from a 2-year college, or have enrolled in or graduated from a 4-year college. However, these breakouts yield cell sizes too small to analyze, with many cells containing only 1-4 percent of the sample. That is, while it might be more accurate to include more than the seven categories described in Table 2, the data do not allow for it.

Independent variables

Below, variables are identified in bold, followed by a discussion of each variable. See also Table 3 (below). Family relationships are analyzed in three dimensions: opportunities for family interaction, the tone of interactions, and their substance.

Measures of opportunities indicate, among other things, how much time parents have on average to interact with children. I examine **family structure**: *are two biological parents present?* And **siblings**: *are more than two children present in the household?* James Coleman (who provides the theoretical foundation for this study), and others have argued that the number of parents and children in the home can influence the number of hours each parent has to dedicate to each child, supporting or limiting each parent's investment in each child's education. I also analyzed **family routines**: *does the household share routines, such as dinners, chores, or celebrations?* However, this variable yielded minimal results. This was surprising given previous analyses and interviews that have suggested the value of family routines, but it is certainly possible that the NLSY97 variable of routines simply did not capture the most important aspects of family routines. For this reason, discussion of the routines variable is largely omitted from the book, but it should be noted that it is controlled for in analyses of opportunities for family interaction.

Turning to tone, Coleman argued that strong parent-child relationships were vital for parents to effectively foster children's strengths and facilitate their educational success. I investigate **parent support**: *do youth feel supported by parents?* This variable combines five individual measures into a scale, including how often parents help youth to do things that are important to them, praise youth for doing well, cancel plans with youth for no good reason (reverse coded), blame youth for their problems (reverse coded), and criticize youth or their ideas (reverse coded). I also examine **responsive *and* directive parenting**: *do parents practice a combination of responsive and directive parenting, fully engaging with children?* Or do they practice neither/either responsive and/or directive parenting? This variable is included in the NLSY97 with responsiveness measured by whether youth report that parents are very supportive, somewhat supportive, or not very supportive, and directiveness determined by whether youth report that parents are strict about making sure they do what they are supposed to do.

Turning to substance, I begin with **family conversations**: *how often do youth ask parents for advice about school or job decisions, or discuss goals and aspirations?* This variable combines (into a scale) youth's reports of how often they asked parents for advice or help on education, training, or job decisions, and how much parents know about their goals and aspirations in life. I also analyze **parent involvement**: *how involved are parents in youth's academic and social lives—do they know youth's friends, friends' parents, teachers, whereabouts, and school activities?* Finally, I analyze **enriching environments**: *does the family provide an enriching environment, such as the opportunity to take classes (e.g., music, dance, foreign language) or use a computer or dictionary at home?* Even when parents lack first-hand information about the education system (as first-generation students' parents do), conversations about goals and aspirations may help keep children focused, monitoring children's day-to-day interactions and activities may help keep children on track, and creating an enriching environment may make up for some of the knowledge parents lack by providing access to knowledge through books, computers, or classes.

Some of these variables are scales. Most scales were created for the NLSY97 by Child Trends Inc., which determined each scale to have acceptable reliability (with coefficients generally between 0.71 and 0.85). I created the scale for family conversations, which has a reliability coefficient of 0.73.

As noted in the book, educational success is also contingent upon students' aptitude; possessing strong cognitive abilities is likely another asset for first-generation students. While previous research has found first-generation students have typically lower SAT scores and are less well academically prepared than are college legacies, their cognitive abilities may nonetheless distinguish them from no-college legacies. Therefore, the study considers *aptitude* with the Armed Services Vocational Aptitude Battery (ASVAB), a standard test of cognitive ability. While the primary aim of the study is to identify how the families of first-generation and college legacy students differ from the families of no-college legacies, addressing differences in aptitude is important if any causal inference is to be considered.

Finally, the study includes several controls. *Cohort* (whether youth were age 13 or 14 in 1997), *race/ethnicity* (non-Hispanic Black, Hispanic, and Asian/American Indian/other compared with non-Hispanic White), *immigrant status* (whether youth were born outside the United States, or whether their parents were born outside the United States), family *income-to-poverty ratio* (the ratio of total annual family income as compared to the Federal poverty level in that year), *parent education* (measured by children's residential mother or father's highest year of education, whomever's is higher), and *gender* (female compared with male).

TABLE 3 • Independent Variables

Concepts	Measures
Oppor-tunities	**Structure**—two-biological parents at home (compared to other family structures), 2000 **Siblings**—>2 children living in the home (i.e., people aged <18 in the home, compared to ≤2), 2000 **Routines**—days/week youth share various family routines, 2000
Tone	**Support**—created variable of parent-youth supportive relationship (including how often parents praise youth for doing well, criticize youth or their ideas, help youth do things that are important to them, blame youth for their problems, and make plans with youth and cancel for no good reason), 1999 **Responsive *and* directive**—do parents practice a combination of responsive *and* directive parenting, or do they practice either or neither? 2000
Substance	**Conversations**—how often youth asked residential parents for advice or help on education, training, or job decisions, and how much parents know about youth's goals and aspirations in life, 2002 **Involvement**—created variable of whether parents get to know youth's friends, friends' parents, teachers; who they are with when not at home; what they are doing in school, 2000 **Enriching environment**—whether youth take classes (e.g., music, dance, foreign language) in a typical week and the home has a computer or dictionary, 1997
Controls	**Cohort**—whether youth are age 13 or 14 on 12/31/96 **Gender**—male, female **Race/ethnicity**—White, Black, Hispanic, Asian/American Indian/other **Family income-to-poverty ratio**— ratio of income to Federal poverty level, 2002 **Parent education**—years of education **First-generation immigrant**—youth born outside the US **Second-generation immigrant**—youth's parents born outside the US **Aptitude**: the Armed Services Vocational Aptitude Battery, 1997

Analysis

Descriptive statistics

The study includes descriptive statistics for the entire NLSY97 sample (ages 12-16 in 1997, ages 22-26 in 2007). While family relationship variables are only available for the 13 and 14 year-old cohorts, postsecondary paths are analyzed for the entire sample, providing a wider span of ages to gain understanding into diverse postsecondary paths. Analyses look at the proportion of youth that reach each level of education—GED recipients and high school graduates, two- and four-year college enrollees, and certificate and degree completers—all broken down by gender, race/ethnicity, family income-to-poverty ratio, and parent education (see Chapter 3). Descriptive analyses are weighted to account for NLSY97 oversampling of non-Hispanic Black and Hispanic youth. This is the only portion of the analysis that includes the entire NLSY97 sample; all regressions are performed using only the 13 and 14 year-old cohorts.

Missing data

With regard to missing data, 23 percent of the sample has no missing data, while 77 percent of the sample is missing data for at least one variable. To address missing data, multiple imputation was performed using a Markov Chain Monte Carlo procedure with Gibbs sampling. In brief, missing data are predicted five times using observed data on other variables for a given youth, as well as observed data for other youth on the missing variable. Every variable described above was utilized to predict missing data, along with data for family relationships collected in other years and additional potentially relevant variables. Missing data are assumed to be missing at random (MAR); that is, it is assumed values can be predicted for missing data using observed data. Following imputation, the five complete (imputed) data sets were analyzed in unison using Stata's "mim" function, resulting in a single set of analysis results.

Multinomial logistic regression analysis

The study largely employs multinomial logistic regression. The baseline regression model includes background variables (cohort, gender, race/ethnicity, immigrant status, parent education, family income-to-poverty ratio, and aptitude, see Table 3, above). In adding family relationships to the model, measures of opportunities are included first, then tone, then substance:

Opportunities: $\log(\pi_j/\pi_J) = \beta_{0j} + \beta_{1j}$(background controls) $+\beta_{2j}$(two parents) $+\beta_{3j}$(siblings) $+\beta_{4j}$(routines)

Tone: $\log(\pi_j/\pi_J) = \beta_{0j} + \beta_{1j}$(background controls) $+\beta_{2j}$(supportive parenting) $+\beta_{3j}$(engaged parenting)

Substance: $\log(\pi_j/\pi_J) = \beta_{0j} + \beta_{1j}$(background controls) $+\beta_{2j}$(involved parenting) $+\beta_{3j}$(family conversations) $+\beta_{4j}$(enriching environments)

Next, regressions build incrementally towards the fullest model, beginning by adding measures of opportunities, followed by the addition of tone, then substance:

$\log(\pi_j/\pi_J) = \beta_{0j} + \beta_{1j}$(background controls) $+\beta_{2j}$(two parents) $+\beta_{3j}$(siblings) $+\beta_{4j}$(routines) $+\beta_{5j}$(supportive parenting) $+\beta_{6j}$(engaged parenting) $+\beta_{7j}$(involved parenting) $+\beta_{8j}$(family conversations) $+\beta_{9j}$(enriching environments)

I build the regression analyses in this order to examine the interrelated nature of opportunities, tone, and substance. As discussed in the main text, opportunities for family interaction might matter, in part, because they lay a vital foundation for tone and substance. Spending time together provides a setting in which supportive and engaged parent-child relationships may develop, and in which substantive conversations and interactions may take place. Therefore, it is possible that opportunities bear less significance when measures of tone and substance are added to regressions. In turn, tone may matter, in part, because it affects the kinds of conversations and interactions families are able to share. Supportive and engaged family relationships might matter partly because they open the doors to more substantive family conversations and interactions. Thus, the tone of family relationships could carry less sway when measures of substance are included in regressions.

To model this, I first examine whether opportunities predict tone, and whether tone predicts substance. I find that measures of opportunities for family interaction significantly predict the tone of family interactions. In fact, in regressions controlling for all background characteristics, each measure of opportunity for interaction significantly predicts both supportive and engaged parenting.

Further extending the argument, the tone of family interactions also significantly predicts the substance of interactions: in regressions controlling for all background characteristics, both supportive and engaged parenting significantly predict parent involvement, frequent family conversations about education and goals, and an enriching environment. This aligns with the idea that substantive interactions are more likely to occur if parents and children share supportive and engaged relationships.

Finally, I examine whether family influence rests on a foundation of opportunities, which allows a supportive and engaged tone to emerge, in the context of which substantive communications are more likely to occur, all to the benefit of children's educations—that is, I examine whether there is "mediation." Indeed, the effect of opportunities for family interaction is modestly reduced when the tone of family interactions is added to the model. And adding measures of substance to the model modestly reduces the effect of both opportunities and tone. It appears that part of the reason that opportunities for family interaction matter for educational attainment is that the tone of family interactions tends to be more beneficial in families with more opportunities for interaction. Further, part of the reason that opportunities for and the tone of family interactions matter for education is that the substance of family interactions tends to be more advantageous in families with more opportunities for interaction and a more supportive, engaged tone. While opportunities and tone typically remain significant even when measures of substance are included in the model, it seems that a portion of their role is indeed in laying a sound foundation on which substantive interactions may emerge.

While the effect of each facet of family relationships (i.e., opportunities, tone, and substance) is reduced by adding another aspect of family relationships to the model (indicating a mediating relationship), this mediation is quite modest, and measures of family relationships generally remain significant even when the full spectrum of family relationship variables is analyzed within a single model. It appears that the three facets of family relationships also each individually support education.

Multinomial logistic regression requires Independence of Irrelevant Alternatives (IIA). This means that all categories (college legacy, no-college legacy, first-generation, and downwardly mobile; four-year college, some-college, and no college) must be meaningfully distinct; pairs of odds must be determined without reference to the other response categories. The Hausman test formally tests IIA—by excluding one category at a time and investigating whether coefficients are significantly different. The Hausman test confirms IIA for all dependent variables analyzed herein.

Multicollinearity is another potential issue among variables of family relationships. Using Stata's "estat vif" command, I verified that multicollinearity is not a problem for variables of family relationships analyzed in the study.

Finally, most measures of family relationships in the NLSY97 were collected in 1997 and the early 2000s. The second point of data collection for measures of family relationships varies—variables were re-collected in 2000 (when youth were ages 16-17), 2001 (when youth were 17-18), or 2002 (when youth were ages 18-19). Unfortunately, two measures were only collected at one point in time—the measure of enriching environments is only available in early-adolescence, and the measure of conversations is only available in late-adolescence.

To take advantage of the NLSY97's longitudinal data, when the same concept was measured on two occasions, each regression was performed twice, examining early- and late-adolescent data alternatively. (Unfortunately, regressions including both early- and late-adolescent data in the same model suffered from multicollinearity, an issue that often arises when some variables are lagged versions of others). Thus, the study was able to examine whether family relationships are particularly pivotal to first-generation success at one of these times. It seemed possible that early-adolescent choices could be especially important for first-generation success, as behaviors and attitudes established in early-adolescence might have continuing importance over time. It could also be that late-adolescent choices are most significant, as they mark the period when first-generation youth must forge new ground by applying to, gaining acceptance at, and enrolling in college. However, a strong pattern did not emerge; findings were similar for early- and late-adolescent family relationships. For that reason, only late-adolescent data are presented in the book (with one exception, noted by footnote).

Acknowledgements

I would like to thank my Dad for making the dream of writing this book a reality. You've supported my love of writing and my passion for promoting equality for as long as I can remember. I am continually inspired by your encouragement and example.

I am also grateful for the guidance and support of my dissertation chair Dr. Stefanie DeLuca; dissertation reader Dr. Karl Alexander; and thorough and thoughtful edits from Laurie Harrison and Linda Blaydon.

Finally, to Steve: here's to supporting our children's dreams together. I love you.

About the Authors

Dr. Elizabeth Dayton holds B.A. and M.A. degrees from Stanford University, and a Ph.D. from Johns Hopkins University. She focused her studies on psychology and sociology, and in particular on how families influence educational outcomes. The research presented in this book was funded by an American Educational Research Association Dissertation Grant supported by the National Science Foundation (under grant #DRL-0941014; opinions are the authors' and do not necessarily reflect those of the granting agencies). Following her doctorate, Elizabeth returned to Stanford University as a postdoctoral fellow.

Charles Dayton holds a B.A. from Binghamton University, and M.A.s from Syracuse University and San Jose State University. He focused his studies on literature and psychology. He worked at a national research institute in Palo Alto for twelve years where he focused on education and health issues, and led a group at the University of California at Berkeley for thirteen years to improve educational and career outcomes for youth from low-income families. He has also written three mysteries, a book of short stories, and a novel.

Together they provide an unusual team: a daughter-father collaboration working to present relevant research in a highly readable form.

www.ingramcontent.com/pod-product-compliance
Lightning Source LLC
Chambersburg PA
CBHW070959040426
42443CB00007B/585

* 9 7 8 0 9 9 7 9 4 6 7 0 3 *